First edition
Copyright © 2009 Alastair Sawday Publishing Co. Ltd
Published in 2009

Alastair Sawday Publishing Co. Ltd,
The Old Farmyard, Yanley Lane,
Long Ashton, Bristol BS41 9LR, UK
Tel: +44 (0)1275 395430
Web: www.sawdays.co.uk

ISBN-13: 978-1-906136-18-5

Series editor: Alastair Sawday
Editorial Director: Annie Shillito
Editor: Jackie King
Editorial Assistance: Florence Oldfield
Writing: Alastair Sawday, Jackie King
Production: Julia Richardson, Rachel Coe,
Tom Germain; Anny Mortada
Maps: Maidenhead Cartographic Services
Printing: Printer Trento, Italy
Cover photograph: Atlantide Phototravel/Corbis
Cover design: Walker Jansseune

Photography

Mark Bolton
La Traversina Agriturismo
Agriturismo Cascina Folletto
B&B Valferrara
La Piana dei Castagni Agriturismo
Antica Casa 'Le Rondini'
Tenuta di Pieve a Celle
Fattoria Barbialla Nuova
Sovigliano
Locanda Casanuova
Azienda Agricola Le Tore
Lama di Luna - Biomasseria
Masseria Serra dell'Isola
Masseria Il Frantoio
Masseria Impisi
San Teodoro Nuovo Agriturismo
Hotel Villa Schuler
Hotel Signum

Lucy Pope
Agriturismo Cervano B&B
Ca' del Rocolo
Agriturismo La Faula
Casa del Grivò
La Sosta di Ottone III
Agriturismo Rendola Riding
Relais San Pietro in Polvano
La Locanda
Frances' Lodge
Podere Salicotto
Il Rigo
Podere Le Mezzelune
Pieve di Caminino
Locanda della Valle Nuova
Locanda del Gallo
Casa San Gabriel
Villa Aureli
La Palazzetta del Vescovo
I Mandorli Agriturismo
La Torretta

Helena Smith
Villa Michaela
Le Due Volpi
Villa Campestri
Casa Palmira
Azienda Agricola Il Borghetto
Fattoria Viticcio Agriturismo
Odina Agriturismo
Fattoria Tregole

Ross James
Il Pardini's Hermitage

*We had long been mulling over the Slow books, but somehow couldn't magic up the right formula. Jo Boissevain, our copy editor
and writer, took a book dummy to her artist husband. Together they concocted such a winning title and initial cover idea that they
breathed new life into a recumbent body. Go Slow England was the first book in the series and this is the second.*

Go Slow Italy

Alastair Sawday
with Jackie King

Foreword
by Giorgio Locatelli

Special places to stay

SWITZERLAND

HUNGARY

FRIULI-
VENEZIA-
GIULIA

48
44

SLOVENIA

Bergamo

36

LOMBARDY Brescia

VENETO

CROATIA

Milan

40

Vicenza Mestre

Verona

Venice

Padua

TURIN (TURINO)

Mantua

Cremona

PIEDMONT

Piacenza

32
28

Parma

Ferrara

BOSNIA-
HERZEGOVINA

Reggio nell'Emilia

Modena

EMILIA-ROMAGNA

LIGURIA

GENOA
(GENOVA)

52

Bologna

FRANCE

60

56

SAN REMO

Mediterranean Sea

86
90 82

70 74 78

Florence

Livorno

TUSCANY

102 110 114

94 98 106 118

126 122

130

146

134

138

150 142

154

164

168

172

Perugia

MARCHE

176

UMBRIA 184

180

188

Ancona

*Adriatic
Sea*

LAZIO

ROME

202

Bari

PUGLIA 206 214

210

CAMPANIA

NAPLES

Potenza

BASILICATA 218

198

Tyrrhenian Sea

*Golfo di
Taranto*

226

PALERMO

Messina

222

SICILY

Catania

Syracuse

*Ionian
Sea*

Contents

7   Foreword by Giorgio Locatelli
8   Introduction by Alastair Sawday

The North
22   Maps and regional information

28   La Traversina Agriturismo, Piedmont
32   Agriturismo Cascina Folletto, Piedmont
36   Agriturismo Cervano B&B, Lombardy
40   Ca' del Rocolo, Veneto
44   Agriturismo La Faula, Friuli-Venezia-Giulia
48   Casa del Grivò, Friuli-Venezia-Giulia
52   B&B Valferrara, Emilia-Romagna
56   La Piana dei Castagni Agriturismo, Emilia-Romagna
60   La Sosta di Ottone III, Liguria

Tuscany
64   Maps and regional information

70   Villa Michaela, Tuscany
74   Antica Casa 'Le Rondini', Tuscany
78   Tenuta di Pieve a Celle, Tuscany
82   Le Due Volpi, Tuscany
86   Villa Campestri, Tuscany
90   Casa Palmira, Tuscany
94   Fattoria Barbialla Nuova, Tuscany
98   Sovigliano, Tuscany
102   Azienda Agricola Il Borghetto, Tuscany
106   Fattoria Viticcio Agriturismo, Tuscany
110   Locanda Casanuova, Tuscany
114   Odina Agriturismo, Tuscany
118   Agriturismo Rendola Riding, Tuscany
122   Relais San Pietro in Polvano, Tuscany
126   La Locanda, Tuscany
130   Fattoria Tregole, Tuscany

134   Frances' Lodge, Tuscany
138   Podere Salicotto, Tuscany
142   Il Rigo, Tuscany
146   Podere le Mezzelune, Tuscany
150   Pieve di Caminino, Tuscany
154   Il Pardini's Hermitage, Tuscany

Central
158   Maps and regional information

164   Locanda della Valle Nuova, Le Marche
168   Locanda del Gallo, Umbria
172   Casa San Gabriel, Umbria
176   Villa Aureli, Umbria
180   La Palazzetta del Vescovo, Umbria
184   I Mandorli Agriturismo, Umbria
188   La Torretta, Lazio

The South
192   Maps and regional information

198   Azienda Agricola Le Tore, Campania
202   Lama di Luna – Biomasseria, Puglia
206   Masseria Serra dell'Isola, Puglia
210   Masseria Il Frantoio, Puglia
214   Masseria Impisi, Puglia
218   San Teodoro Nuovo Agriturismo, Basilicata
222   Hotel Villa Schuler, Sicily
226   Hotel Signum, Salina, Aeolian Islands

230   Italy by train
232   Italy on a bike
234   Sawday's Fragile Earth series
236   Sawday's Special Places to Stay series
239   Index

Foreword by Giorgio Locatelli

"Food inspires conviviality and it is central to all that is Slow. I remember the lovely atmosphere at mealtimes at home in Italy when I was little – the sense that everyone had come together to join in with the preparation of a meal. My grandmother would be stirring something, my mother chopping, my grandfather grating the parmesan and I would lay the table. Everyone played a role. I learnt about cooking, too, especially their respect for good ingredients, and I absorbed a lot of knowledge.

I always ask my children to help at home because I want them, too, to have that sense of creating something together. Mealtimes are important for families.

Sometimes when friends invite me for supper, I can see that they are really stressed – there is smoke coming out of the kitchen and their hair is on end. I hate to see that. I would rather that they just put out a nice piece of cheese, some bread and some wine, then we could all relax. Spending time with people is the important thing, not what you eat.

Lots of people have this idea that food is a problem and they sigh when they wonder what to cook for supper. You don't find that in Italy. Nobody minds the little bit of work because they love the end result, the bit where they stop and sit down together. Food seems to bring more happiness in Italy than anywhere else.

The Slow Movement is reconnecting people with their regional culture – I am totally in tune with it and so are the people in this book. They can work a special magic for you."

Giorgio Locatelli
Chef proprietor of Locanda Locatelli
www.locandalocatelli.com

Introduction by Alastair Sawday

Its time has come. 'Slow' is upon us and it is the least controversial 'new' idea I have ever embraced. Who can argue against it, especially if lying in a hammock after a good lunch with friends in Italy? As the heat settles like a blanket over the soft browns of the landscape, you haven't the heart to give yourself a hard time.

That is one view of Slow: harmless idleness, eating and drinking good and honestly produced food and wine, enjoying good conversation and convivial company. But, of course, below the placid surface of that picture swirl the turbulent currents of food politics, competing production systems, attitudes to progress, global struggles for trade dominance, land ownership and more. Slow is a political movement; it is in deadly earnest, a powerful idea with the capacity for changing the way we think and act. Peaceful and non-confrontational, but reaching deep into our lives, it has some of the underlying power of Ghandi's revolutionary pacifism. But before we take ourselves too seriously let us go back to the foundations of it all.

Have you ever eaten a McDonald's hamburger? I confess that I have, once. I have even lunched in the canteen of the McDonald's Hamburger University near Chicago. I think that was its official name, and it still trains employees to 'believe in' hamburgers, and McDonald's. Brilliantly effective, and heart-breakingly fatuous. If it were just clever and silly we would have little to worry about. But of course it is much, much more than that.

Carlo Petrini, an Italian food journalist, was so saddened to see that a McDonald's had opened near the Spanish Steps in Rome, one of Europe's most iconic and beautiful cities, that he resolved to battle the growth of Fast Food with its logical alternative – Slow Food. He had seen how fast food had threatened to undermine much of Italy's traditional food-production, had driven young people into the arms of an alien and damaging culture, fattened them and filled them with junk. Much that he loved about his country was under threat from this invasion of shallow, industrial food marketing. He saw it as the thin end of a long and dangerous wedge. Luckily he had hit upon an idea with its own momentum and commercial potential.

Back in Bra, a small town not far from Turin in northern Italy, Carlo Petrini created the Slow Food Movement and launched a series of devastating attacks on the way that his country,

with others, had allowed itself to be duped into accepting fast food. Far more powerfully, he encouraged people to think of Slow Food as a

creative and wholly enjoyable phenomenon. This part wasn't difficult. Suddenly, those who had always been happy to pay a bit more for food grown well, by local people, were made to feel part of something bigger and more significant. Pig farmers who rejected factory farming, raised their pigs in the forest, fattened them on acorns and apples and refused to feed them unnecessarily on hormones and antibiotics – they were now serious players in a movement that celebrated them. They were never going to get rich, but not all of us want to. For people who like doing things their own way, the Slow movement has been a tonic.

I wrote an article on Slow for the Guardian a while ago, and a couple of paragraphs fit neatly here:

"When horses pulled carriages and charabancs, when bicycles were considered dangerous beasts, when flags were waved from rooftops to pass on news, there were always

people who were nevertheless considered 'fast'. Young men galloped insanely quickly on their horses, gambled their money away and drank too much. Cities have always encouraged fast living, whatever the century.

However, our western societies have slowly and almost imperceptibly learned to live at a pace that would have alarmed even those insanely galloping young men. We need, it seems, to be 'elsewhere', anywhere but 'here'. Holidays have to be far away, the further the better. Food comes from distant countries; friends are cultivated beyond our immediate reach; we work hard in order to have time not to work. So it goes on. But there is hope. The Slow movement is also, as it were, gathering speed, and it will affect the way we holiday and possibly everything else too. It is more serious than it sounds.

To the oldest among us, these ideas are merely new feet in old socks. There is nothing

new about taking it easy, keeping your own chickens, holidaying at home, enjoying your friends. But for the rest these ideas need to be

re-articulated and spread, for we are so caught up in the modern world of speed that we have lost our perspective. For some of us, life only seems to have much meaning if we are planning to fly off on holiday. What else is there?"

Well, the Slow movement can give us meaning, a conceptual framework into which we

can fit ideas that range more widely. In Italy there began the CittaSlow – Slow City – movement in response to the modern obsession with speed. Some of those languidly lovely Tuscan hilltop towns, such as Greve in Chianti, began to bed Slow ideas into town planning and governance. Why not encourage Slow production methods by giving priority to artisans? Why pollute the sky with street lighting when it could be directed downwards? Why not give people priority over cars, allow public transport to serve the public? In many towns the local Slow Food chapters have seen off bad planning applications.

Cynics might suggest that the Slow movement is bound to thrive in Italy, of all places, because everything moves at a crawl

there anyway. Try getting the bureaucracy to shift, a phone installed or planning permission granted. Is Slow merely making a virtue out of the inevitable? However, another view is that Italians can get things done at high speed when they need to, often just ignoring the system that lies in the way. Perhaps Slow thrives there because Italians are so happy to ignore the rules; the Health and Safety regime is, of course, anti-Slow because it insists on new and complex ways of doing old, well-tried, things.

The reach of Slow ideas is enormous – into energy, food security, the way old people are treated and children taught, waste is handled and houses built. Slow cities are booming in Italy, though they are usually 'towns'. In the UK we have a few too – Ludlow, Dereham, Aylsham, Diss, Mold, Berwick, Cockermouth, Perth and Linlithgow – and they are thriving. It appears that people want to live in them. It is obvious, isn't it?

It is indeed obvious, but not so obvious that we all get the message. I went to a play in Bristol last year in which the frantic madness of our obsession with movement, change and speed was played out on stage. Young executives, plugged into their mobiles and laptops, walked on conveyor belts, rolled around at speed on their executive chairs, were gaily caught up in a clashing kaleidoscope of technology and optimism. They were going nowhere, but were exhilarated by the journey. Standing back and taking a look was not an option.

This introduction is perhaps not a place to be too serious, but I can't pass by without saying why, beyond all other reasons, I am keen to promote Slow ideas. It is because they go far, far deeper than it might seem. They embrace the vastness of the ecological crisis that is threatening us all. While we are taking fossil fuels from the ground and recklessly burning them at irretrievable cost to the planet, those who adopt a Slow approach are burning less. While globalisation creates inconceivable wealth for a few and impoverishes many, a Slow economy acknowledges the need for local solutions and restraint. I won't press on with this argument here, but I did want to touch on it. Slow is serious too. And it is sophisticated, as the recent international banking crisis might suggest.

So, perhaps one can describe Slow as a bridge from panic to pleasure. Out of distressing awareness Slow brings hope. Others may be hell-bent on destroying the planet but if we eat that locally reared pig, drink organic wine from the region, buy our bread from the baker and stay in Europe for our holidays, then we are acting, and perhaps being, positive. If we want to think of it that way, we are even being radical.

I have just mentioned organics, which brings me to another reason for embracing Slow. At work celebrations we try to eat only organic food; no other form of quality control really works at such a demanding level. Organic agriculture provides an impressive package of benefits: lower pollution rates, increased habitat for wildlife, higher employment levels, lower fossil-fuel use, community stability – and so on. A partnership between the Organic and Slow movements was inevitable. The former works at creating the highest standards and ensuring that they are maintained; the latter is less demanding, wider-ranging and gets closer to people's hearts. There is no such thing as a Slow grower, just a grower who likes Slow ideas. Nobody polices his performance, but that is why the movement has grown so dramatically. It is an Idea – a sophisticated justification for continuing to do things the old way, or a platform for serious thinking. It is – and this is very appealing to Italians – an honour system.

Now I come to Italy... When we published *Go Slow England*, our best-selling book in 2008, we knew that the fun would continue when we took on Italy for our next project. *Go Slow Italy* has been a book-in-waiting. Here the Slow Food movement began, here the loss of traditional ways of growing food, eating and drinking, living in communities has been slower than elsewhere in western Europe. That is why we go there in such numbers, year after year, decade after decade. Italy remains lovably resistant to the clarion calls of 'progress'. They do progress

well when they want to, but there beats in the heart of every Italian a preference for human beings over systems and over commerce and speed. Yes, they are keen on 'la bella figura', not a very Slow notion, but it is fairly harmless and undermines any obsession with ideas that have more complex expression, and unintended consequences – like efficiency and success.

Searching among our Special Places to Stay in Italy for the ones that are genuinely Slow was a delightful task. Choosing those to include here was difficult. Growing their own food? Taking it easy after rejecting hectic lives? Spending half the day preparing great food and the other half eating it? This is what lucky Italians do. They always have. It is hard to go to any corner of Italy without encountering the ancient Romans, epicures and lovers of the Good Life when they weren't battling barbarians. I love, beyond almost anywhere, the Italian lakes. Around Lake Como are the remains of some gorgeous villas to which rich Romans would retire to write their memoirs or enjoy lives of ease and good food. They rarely retired abroad, knowing that Italy was where life could be well lived.

Italians still stay largely in Italy. They take their holidays there, they retire there. Why do the English retire and holiday abroad in huge numbers? It can't just be the weather. Maybe it is also because they are, often unconsciously, seeking a Slow life. They like people talking to them in the street, even if they resent it at home. They love taking their time over meals and eating with others, even if they rarely do at home. They admire the way Italians

have kept their small shops, though they flock to Tesco like lemmings at home.

Have we, in England and elsewhere, lost so much that what we have lost is seen as nostalgia rather than as part of our reality? Have we destroyed so many town centres that we can no longer imagine a beautiful one as part of our lives? We have erected so many brutally ugly buildings that we now see them as inevitable, perhaps. Italy has retained so much that is beautiful that they see beauty, I believe, as their birthright. Slow has its roots in a love of beauty. It is fundamentally an aesthetic movement. It cannot thrive where ugliness rules.

This book is titled Go Slow Italy because it is about far more than Slow Food. It invites you to get there slowly, stay awhile, to float serenely through the days – conversing, enjoying every experience rather than longing for whatever might be over the next hill. It invites intimacy, simplicity.

You will discover some lovely people in this book, people who have made the sort of life-changing decisions that we only dream about. If you have dreamed of abandoning the rat-race, you will enjoy meeting those who have done it. Rather than embracing conventional 'progress',

then inevitable frustration with bureaucratic inertia, they have adopted Slow as a life-enhancing form of progress.

Slow Travel is part of the new Slow Movement, as are slow sex, slow business, slow everything. And how we need it! We have an inalienable right to travel – which nowadays means fast travel – under the UN Declaration of Human Rights. The UN in 2001 even declared that 'obstacles should not be placed in the way of... participation in international tourism'. So it is hardly surprising, if you add the seductivity of the budget airlines, that we gad about all over the world as if there were no consequences. Well, the consequences are vast

and are coming home to roost. I won't go into total 'eco' mode, for you are here now to enjoy the best of Italian Slow, but do remember that by adopting Slow ideas you are playing out a new and positive role. You are, even, part of a subtle but powerful revolution. If it keeps McDonald's at bay, it will have achieved something.

If this book tempts you out of your armchair, look up these special places on our website to find lots more useful information. And, when you travel to Italy, don't forget to travel slowly – by train. We've given the nearest train station for each place and, at the back of the book, there are features on getting about by train and bike.

How to be *fast.*

Take taxis, not buses

Say 'yes' to every invitation

Tumble-dry clothes, even in summer

Drive to the supermarket to buy a ready meal

Take your laptop on holiday

Move to New York

Text your teenagers upstairs to tell them to turn down the music

Buy quick-cook pasta

Ask someone how they are while busying yourself with what you are doing

Turn on your mobile as soon as you get out of bed

Know that the weather has no bearing on your day

Own a BlackBerry

Rarely call your family

Plan your holiday around cheap flights

Work miles from home

Hothouse your kids in a fast-track school

Buy a kid's story tape instead of a book

Use a microwave

Answer your mobile regardless of who you are with and where you are

Squeeze your time so much that you have to drive to everything

Expect instant service and gratification for everything and anything you want

Confine your reading to magazines, blogs and celebrity news

Only see films playing in multiplexes

Smoke – and support the tobacco industry

Buy kindling from the garage

Ignore the stuff in the fridge and get a take-away

Feel the need to be on Facebook past the age of 30

Shove the dog into the garden instead of going for a walk

Buy your child a quad bike

Change your décor before it goes out of fashion

Drink to escape

Buy ready-cut fruit in a plastic container

Hurl all your rubbish together into a big black bin liner

Drive around the gym looking for the closest space to the entrance

Make so many appointments that you always feel stretched

Tune in to a radio play

Check emails only twice a day

Write a letter to your mother/sister/best friend
and post it

Cook to music

Learn to say 'no'

Plan your days around large, communal meals

In your spare time, eat, sleep
and rest when your body
tells you to

Let the cat have a nap on your lap

How to be
Slow...

Make your own stock, soups
and sauces

Learn to meditate

Get acquainted with your local buses

Teach your children
to cook

Spend time with a baby

Bake a cake

Learn to fly fish

Make a scrapbook for your grown-up children out
of your memories of their childhood

Plant a tree that is going to be fully
grown long after you are gone

Play a board game

Write a diary

Argue about the best way
to cook rib of beef

Get to know your butcher, baker
and greengrocer

Borrow dvds and cds from
the library

Light the fire and
turn off the TV

Have suppers,
not dinner parties

Get passionate about pork belly

Buy a bike – and ride it

Work from home some of
the week

Ask your parents to tell you about
their childhood

Take a toddler for a walk

Buy only what you need and don't be a
slave to marketing

Piedmont   Lombardy   Veneto

Friuli-Venezia-Giulia   Emilia-Romagna   Liguria

[THE NORTH]

THE NORTH

The rich and powerful north is closer to the rest of Europe in many ways and, with France, Switzerland, Austria and Slovenia at its borders, it has a multi-cultural feel. It is a huge Alpine area stretching from the Golfo di Genova in the west to the Golfo di Venezia in the east. To the south, the Po River winds its way through the vast and fertile Lombardy Plain emptying into the Adriatic; the southern border of Emilia-Romagna reaches across the northern range of the Apennines before descending to the flatlands. The cities of the north have drawn people in their droves from the historically poor south in search of jobs.

Piedmont is a border region with its sights turned firmly to Europe, ever receptive to progress yet with more small farms and tiny villages than most regions. It has spawned huge industries such as Fiat and Olivetti and yet is still deeply rooted in tradition and has a strong sense of place.

The Royal House of Savoy made Turin its capital in 1563, triggering a grand period of baroque construction. It is a handsome, elegant and stylish capital city, more French than Italian, with wide streets and a geometric street plan. It regained its crown as a capital when the Kingdom of Italy was united. Turin is well worth a visit during the colder months when the city lives its understated fashionable life. At weekends the locals take off to the mountains - only an hour or so away by train.

Don't miss the fine museums, such as Il Museo Egizo, or a hot chocolate and some freshly-baked *pasticceria* in one of the beautiful portico-ed piazzas. Turin also hosts the bi-ennial *Salone de Gusto*, the internationally-acclaimed Slow Food fair.

In the Piedmont valleys you will find dishes unique to each - each, for example, has its own twist on the *bagna calda*, a fondue made with

"rich and powerful, the north has a multi-cultural feel"

garlic, anchovies and walnut oil served with seasonal vegetables.

Chiavenna, a medieval village to the north of Como in **Lombardy**, has bubbling mountain waters coursing through its centre and surrounding nature parks draw bird-watchers. The towns of Bergamo and Brescia have the most famous piano festival in the world, the Festival Michelangeli.

Venice! No adjective is worthy of her, 'a maiden city bright and free'. Today, tragically, the jewel in **Veneto**'s - the world's? - crown is slowly but inevitably sinking into the sea but her beauty survives: in squares, quiet backwaters and residential *calli* (lanes) where real people live and work just a short hop from heaving Piazza San Marco and the Rialto. An early-morning walk is a good way to get a feel for it all; for real serenity share a silent Basilica di San Marco with those at prayer. Modern art enthusiasts should time their visit to catch Venice's Biennale art show.

Don't overlook Treviso, Padova or Mantova (the latter is just in Lombardy), each as charming as Verona, nor the Veneto countryside, rich in elegant Palladian villas.

The Alpine region of **Friuli-Venezia-Giulia** is a name little known outside Italy. The Friuli part of the name originates from Forum Iuli, named after Julius Caesar, now known at the city of Cividale. Italian, the Friulian language, Slovenian and some German are spoken here.

The clear mountain air, crystal clear waters and sheltered river valleys produce outstanding wines and food: renowned grappa, good meat and trout, San Daniele ham, salamis made from goose and a huge variety of unusual cheeses.

The July Folkfest, held every year, spans 30 towns here and in neighbouring Veneto.

Bologna - '*la rossa, la dotta e la grassa*': 'red' for its politics and its stone, 'learned' because of its academics, 'fat' thanks to its reputation for gastronomy - has the oldest university in Europe and is a handsome, rewarding city. The duomo and its towers are all built of local pink stone and glow red as the light fades and the cobalt sky starts to fill with stars.

There are many fine towns in **Emilia-Romagna** connected by a rail system that runs the width of the region from Piacenza in the west to Ravenna on the Adriatic coast. Ferrara, Modena and Ravenna are all World Heritage sites and many small towns have achieved 'CittaSlow' status.

Much of the region's produce is world-famous - *Prosciutto di Parma, Parmigiano Reggiano, aceto balsamico* - but there is much more to discover including outstanding wines such as Lambrusco Grasparossa di Castelvetro, L'Albana di Romagna DOCG, Sangiovese and Trebbiano.

Liguria is a rainbow-shaped land running around the Gulf of Genoa with a narrow coastal plain dotted with sparkling bays; the land behind rises sharply into towering mountain terrain. Its mild climate earned it a reputation as Europe's flower garden; every bit of contoured fertile land is ringed and stepped with glass houses, vineyards or olive trees. The food is richly interesting: *La torta pasquilina* is filled with rice, vegetables and seasonal wild herbs and *pansooti*, big ravioli, are filled with *preboggion,* a delicate mix of wild herbs. *Taggiasca* olives make the sweetest oil.

The road that links France with Italy disappears deep into long mountain tunnels only to appear again on lofty viaducts high above the sea. Magnificent.

Lindy Wildsmith

THE NORTH

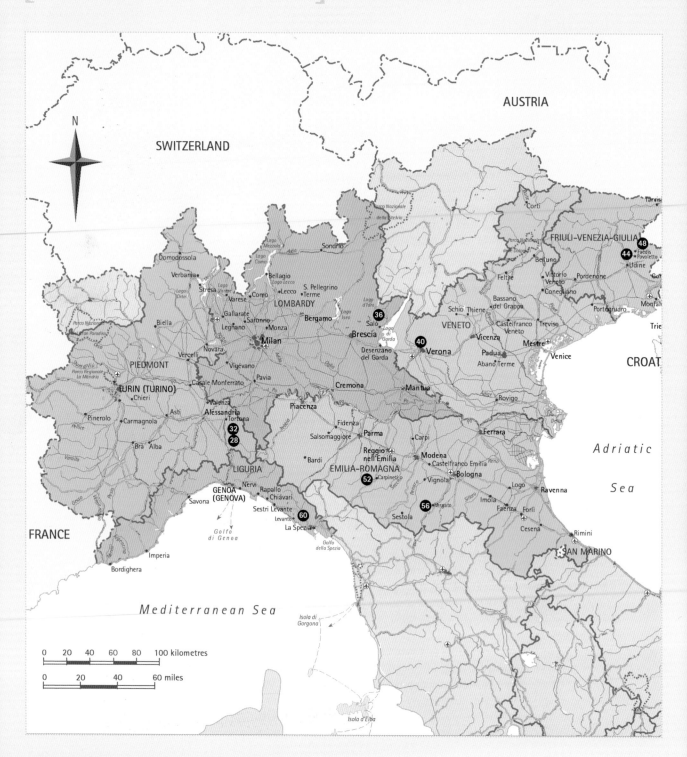

AUSTRIA

SWITZERLAND

N

FRIULI-VENEZIA-GIULIA

Tarvisi

Corti

Belluno
Vittorio
Veneto
Pordenone
Conegliano
Portogruaro
Monfal
Trie

Faedis
Povoletto
Udine
Gor

44 **48**

Domodossola

Verbania

Lago
Mezzola

Sondrio

Parco Nazionale
dello Stelvio

Lago
Como

Bellagio
Lago Lecco

S. Pellegrino
Terme

LOMBARDY

Lago
d'Idro

Parco Nazionale

Feltre

Bassano
del Grappa

Schio Thiene

VENETO

Vicenza

Castelfranco
Veneto

Treviso

Mestre

Venice

CROAT

Stresa
Lago
d'Orta

Como

Varese

Gallarate
Saronno

Legnano
Monza

Bergamo

Lago
d'Iseo

Salò

Lago
di
Garda

Brescia

Desenzano
del Garda

Verona

Padua

Abano Terme

36

40

Biella

Vercelli

Novara

Milan

Vigevano

Pavia

Cremona

Mantua

Rovigo

PIEDMONT

TURIN (TURINO)

Chieri

Casale Monferrato

Valenza

Alessandria

Tortona

Piacenza

Po

Fidenza

Salsomaggiore

Parma

Carpi

Modena

Castelfranco Emilia

Bologna

Ferrara

Adriatic

Sea

Asti

Pinerolo

Carmagnola

Bra Alba

32
28

Bardi

Reggio
nell'Emilia

EMILIA-ROMAGNA

Carpinetro

Vignola

Logo

Imola

Ravenna

Faenza

Forlì

Parco Nazionale
Gran Paradiso

Parco Regionale
la Mandria

LIGURIA

Nervi

Rapallo
Chiavari

Sestri Levante

Levanto

GENOA
(GENOVA)

Savona

52

56

Sestola

Vergato

Cesena

Rimini

Imperia

Bordighera

FRANCE

La Spezia

Golfo
di Genoa

Golfo
della Spezia

60

SAN MARINO

Mediterranean Sea

*Isola di
Gorgona*

Isola d'Elba

Adriatic

Sea

CROAT

0 20 40 60 80 100 kilometres

0 20 40 60 miles

Special places to stay

Piedmont

28 La Traversina Agriturismo

32 Agriturismo Cascina Folletto

Lombardy

36 Agriturismo Cervano B&B

Veneto

40 Ca' del Rocolo

Friuli-Venezia-Giulia

44 Agriturismo La Faula

48 Casa del Grivò

Emilia-Romagna

52 B&B Valferrara

56 La Piana dei Castagni Agriturismo

Liguria

60 La Sosta di Ottone III

La Traversina Agriturismo

PIEDMONT

"I tried being an architect but my heart was too tied to the countryside, to the perfumes of the grasses and the lush woodland, to the fireflies which during the summer nights transform the little valley into an amphitheatre, to the birds and their song. My life here is pure poetry, the poetry of the joy of small but important things. That is why we decided to open our house, to share the joy."

Thus writes Rosanna when asked to describe her journey to this place. She is one of life's 'radiators', radiating joy and life-force in everything she does. She and Domenico really do consider their guests as friends; their attitude to hospitality is shaped by their humanity. There is no talk of 'we and our guests'; it is 'we'. The experience of dining together at their big table is pure 'slow' – convivial, light-hearted, happy, open-minded. "I adore my work. The rhythm of our life and that of our guests is the rhythm of the forest and its animals. This is not pure fancy; I love getting to know new people and sharing with them my passions for flowers, good food, art. After a hard day's work I give thanks that destiny has enabled me to realise my dreams."

For 300 years this house and farm, high on a wooded hillside, have been in Rosanna's family. Was it ever so beautiful and full of life? She gave up a career in architecture to create her version of paradise only 40 minutes from Genoa. If you came for the roses alone you would be happy. One, an attention-seeking star, has climbed all over the front of the house; the air is fragrant with lavender, oregano and roses. But the irises, the hostas, the 230 varieties of plants – they are a magnificent chorus in colourful support. Rosanna has achieved here a level of happiness that is catching. Her exuberance is manifest in the garden, where plants run riot and the feel is, surprisingly, of an English country cottage garden.

The arrival at La Traversina is memorable: Ollie the dog, accompanied by the five cats, may well be the first welcome. You know instantly that you have arrived somewhere special. People love the homely, imaginatively decorated bedrooms with handsome furniture, books and pictures. One visitor wrote of excellent dinners served at a long communal table with friends, guests and family joining in, happily chatting, and enjoying the local produce. She writes: "I was invited to sit at the kitchen table and chat with them while they got dinner under way. Domenico is the perfect foil for spirited Rosanna, who is so organised and efficient that in half an hour she had made a sauce for the pasta, two enormous savoury tarts and two lemon pies, all the while chatting gaily with me."

Vijaya is the young Nepalese Sherpa who is now very much part of the family. He trained as a yoga teacher and they hope soon to create a space in the garden where he will be able to give classes.

Domenico is upholding the desire of Slow Foodies everywhere to protect rare and unusual species of plants. He nurtures a strain of tomatoes that can grow – each one – to an enormous one kilogram! Straw has to be laid beneath each plant to nurture the huge fruit until he decrees it is ready to be harvested – and it is soon on its way to Rosanna's kitchen to be transformed into a delicious dish. All this is part of La Traversina's charm – Rosanna and Domenico have worked a special magic of their own and swept others up into it.

Rosanna & Domenico Varese Puppo

La Traversina Agriturismo,
Cascina La Traversina 109, 15060 Stazzano
- 1 double, 1 family room, €90–€110.
  Half-board €70–€80 p.p. 4 apartments, €115–€135.
- Dinner €25–€32, by arrangement. Wine €7.
- +39 0143 61377
- www.latraversina.com

Agriturismo Cascina Folletto

PIEDMONT

"If it's not in season, it's not on the menu." This simple statement from Andreina sums up her approach to food.

"All the food we cultivate here is organic, and GM-free, naturally, and almost all from old varieties that are protected by the Slow Food Presidium. Around 80% of what we serve is organic and is our own produce; what we can't supply ourselves we buy locally from other farmers and producers who are Slow Food members."

At Cascina Folletto's little restaurant – one that is open to the public – it is a privilege to have Andreina and her mother MariaRosa cooking for you. MariaRosa was born in this 18th-century Tortonese farmhouse.

"I help the guests choose their meal and I explain the ingredients; Mamma does most of the cooking," explains Andreina. "Many of our dishes have a local, historical significance. We have done a lot of research to rediscover forgotten foods and recipes."

The family effort extends to Andrea, Andreina's husband, too. He is a wine specialist and genuinely enjoys telling guests about the local grapes, wines and grappas. He can organise courses, too, for guests who want a deeper understanding of how wines are produced and the flavours achieved.

For him wine is far more than a drink. "Educating people about the wine they have chosen gives them a richer eating experience, a more complete evening. We can introduce them to the *vigneron* – the wine maker – too. I enjoy teaching cookery and particularly like teaching couples. Sometimes we get one partner to prepare the first course and the other to create the second course. Afterwards they will enjoy the meal together on the terrace.

It's a romantic experience for them and they can take the recipes home."

Two crops grown here are of local importance: the wonderful "Scented Strawberries of Tortona" – a Presidia Slow Food – and the Ceci di Merella (chickpeas certified as a Traditional Product of Piedmont). An ancient strain of saffron from the Middle Ages, Scrivia River Valley saffron, is also

> "Many of our dishes have a local, historical significance. We have done a lot of research to rediscover forgotten foods and recipes"

grown. The chickpeas are bottled and preserved to last the whole year. Andreina makes wonderful chickpea foccacia and risottos, too.

There are few producers of the famed Tortona perfumed strawberry – they can be difficult to cultivate and many of the farmers that grew them have retired or died. They are similar to a blackberry, are large, sweet, and unusually scented. They are harvested in one ten-day period each year – usually the second half of June.

A whimsical elf sitting on top of a strawberry is an apt house emblem for Cascina Folletto: once you have tried the fragola profumata you are hooked. No other strawberry will ever satisfy you.

You are encouraged to explore the landscape that gives up all this produce; bikes can be borrowed and trails are discussed. Much of the landscape is surprisingly flat, cultivated agricultural land (a lot of rice is grown in the flatlands of northern Italy).

The nature park at Torrente Scrivia and the Roman city of Libarna are nearby and it's a shortish hop to the coast. They know all the local festivals, events and concerts and take pleasure in

constructing an enticing itinerary for their friends and guests whatever the time of year.

Folletto is a simple farmstead deeply respectful of its place in its community, of its history and traditions. Don't expect luxury laid on specially for you. This is an authentic house with engaging owners, the sort of place that makes you feel you have really got under the skin of Italy – an experience rarely available in hotels.

The farmhouse is, in turns, cheerful and sombre: there is a bright front parlour for tea or coffee, a dining room hung with plates and an upstairs sitting room with balcony views of the fields. A mellow brick archway frames the stone staircase to bedrooms that hold well-polished family furniture, iron-and-walnut beds, brocade spreads, a rocking cot. ('Folletto' has elf-green in its tartan curtains and cushions and is a large suite.)

Tortona is a very ancient town, once an important military station for the Romans. Flattened, stone by stone, by Frederick Barbarossa in 1155, it was then virtually flattened a few more times before finding some sort of peace under the House of Milan and finally of Savoy. Like a dazed boxer, it has survived pummelling from all sides – like so many Italian towns. There are a fine cathedral, a ruined castle and a Roman museum. This is the Italian hinterland – fascinating and rich in its own way, and free from the worst of modern tourism. It is, simply, very 'real'.

Agriturismo Cascina Folletto

strada Veneziana 9/1, fraz. Bettole,
15057 Tortona

- 2 doubles, €80–€100. 1 single, €50.
  1 triple, €110–€120.
- Dinner with wine, €25.
- +39 0143 417224/ +39 339 6749917 (mobile)
- www.cascinafolletto.com
- Train station: Tortona – Novi Ligure

Agriturismo Cervano B&B

LOMBARDY

The Apennines, 150km away, can be seen on a clear day. Does that say something about the air quality? Snow-topped mountains, the deep-blue, glassy Lake Garda and an enormous sky – they are an uplifting spectacle.

Gino and Anna have impeccable eco-credentials and run Cervano with the tiniest impact on their stunning surroundings. Remarkably, too, they have held onto a joie de vivre that is often lost in the quest to live cleanly. "We do all we can to minimise our energy use and as most of our guests are not very green we pass on our tricks to them, too!" says Gino. "I hope they don't think we are being mean, but we simply don't want to waste the earth's resources. We try to live an ecologically responsible life without driving ourselves, and others, mad!"

Gino's words will resonate with those who take the environment seriously. One of the hotel owners from our *Go Slow England* book wrote: "It is not until you set off down the eco road that you realise what a very long road it is."

There are daily dilemmas: which is the most responsible food to buy; balancing your carbon footprint with the need

to run your life efficiently; weighing up one method of heating over another... the list goes on.

The Massaranis have used the most effective insulation, installed 32 square metres of solar panels that supply half the power for the house, use wood from their land to fuel boiler and fires, have a ground-source heat pump and a condensing heating system. Their lighting is light- and movement-sensitive and there are double-glazed windows to keep the heat in. They have won, quite properly, recognition and green certification from ISNART, Italian tourism's Chamber of Commerce.

Avoiding light pollution is an important aspect of the CittaSlow philosophy, and important for wildlife here, too: "Wildlife thrives when we don't flood the land with light - we are surrounded by pheasants, deer, and hare and we want to preserve their natural habitat."

Cervano remains a comfortable villa, an artful restoration of a once-crumbling family home. Built in the 1800s, it is a fine example of Lombard 'fort' design: horses would pull carts laden with hay into the central, narrow, cobblestoned courtyard. Four families once

lived here and many features from the 1800s remain unchanged, such as the lanes and paths to the house and the flow of the mountain spring that irrigates crops of figs, persimmon, apricots, apples, almonds, grapes, nuts, medlars, hazlenuts and tomatoes. Gino and Anna now have two tenths of the original land - the rest has been divided among other family members. "We have the comfort of knowing that the land remains pure. For 100 years it has been cared for organically and we produce the best oil on the Lake - anything from 200-1,000 litres per year."

In 1877 the owners, the Fiorini brothers, channeled the natural springs into two underground pipes, one going to a fountain where barrels from the cellar were washed and another to a marble fountain for washing clothes. They are still there and you'll sometimes spot crayfish that have been carried down from the brook water.

Much, however, has changed inside the house with the arrival of the B&B rooms and self-catering apartments. Only the bathrooms and kitchens have yielded to modern ideas; everything else has been left much as it was at the time of construction. There are slick bathrooms, a marble breakfast bar in a luminous kitchen and decorative floors in a rare, speckled, marble from Verona. Bedrooms are simply and traditionally furnished (one, Monte, is suitable for wheelchair users). One guest wrote "Every morning Gino and Anna would deliver fresh bread and croissants with such a kind touch. They can't do enough for you and, what is more, are immensely knowledgeable about Italian art."

Children are wholeheartedly welcomed; Gino and Anna have even created a hideaway for them in the garden, The Roccolo, a blue 'Smurfs' house that was once a small hunting cottage. "It has two rooms and is for children only, away from the grown-ups," says Gino. He has even crafted pop-guns from elder tree branches that use berries from the laurel as pellets. "We show them how to make the berries bang and smoke." He makes bubble wands from bamboo

canes, too. Paths through the woods are ideal for spotting wildlife: roebucks come to drink in the brook at the back of the villa and fireflies add a sparkle to the garden's night.

"We have created a meditation spot on our small 'mountain' behind the house. The 'Dos' is a little structure flanked with oaks and cypresses and with a terrace onto a spectacular view of the lake."

Mountains and lake are majestic, and the weather is kind; the vast lake creates a micro-climate that helps keep the temperature up, even this far north, and enables farmers to produce the finest olive oils, wines and fruits. The cross-lake ferries are a fun and efficient way of exploring the lake's shores. The endlessly kind Gino and Anna may even take you to local markets and introduce you to their favourite restaurants. You could not be in safer hands or with nicer people. And in the lakes one re-discovers the meaning of beauty.

Gino & Anna Massarini

Agriturismo Cervano B&B,
via Cervano 14, 25088 Toscolano Maderno
- 3 B&B suites, €110-€150;
  4 apartments, from €100 per night.
- Restaurant 1km.
- +39 0365 548398
- www.cervano.com
- Train station: Brescia

Ca' del Rocolo

VENETO

It seems impossibly dreamy, too good to be true. Once upon a time there was a beautiful farm up in the hills above Verona with something to catch the eye at every turn: wooden horses on the terrace, carvings on the walls, flowers on the roof. Children set off to see their friends on horseback, Dad created beautiful objects in his workshop, Mum climbed the hill to collect honey for breakfast. Yet it is all very real, and there is a real streak of steeliness, too, running through Ilaria and Maurizio. This is evident in their determination to be forces for environmental good; their commitment to living responsibly means that while you are with them you'll feel far from the madding excesses of consumer culture.

"Every day we have to make choices that affect us, our guests and the land," says Ilaria. "We spend a lot of time thinking about the right choices. Our electricity comes from a green provider that puts profits into research on renewable energy; we heat the water with solar panels; we reduce our waste, save water and travel only little and responsibly. But we are involved in tourism – albeit in a small way – and that has a huge impact on the environment. Most of our foreign guests arrive by plane and then hire a car – they need one in these hills – and that has a negative impact that cancels out some of our work. But these conflicts are a common part of being aware; if we opted for a career in conservation in a far-off place, we would fly back and forth. We try to do our best and hope to show guests that it's possible to make a difference."

So you will be encouraged to explore the hives, the eight organic hectares and the woodwork studio. The extension - the sala desgustazione, the tasting room - is made from wood and hemp and has a 'living' roof planted with bright flowers; the turf on the roof insulates the room. These living roofs are still pioneering experiments but will one day be

common as we struggle to find more intelligent ways of saving energy and growing food.

The Corazzas are keen supporters of local agriculture. "Our farm is organic and we use as much organic produce as possible but we often choose to buy local – food we trust but which hasn't got an official organic label. The goats cheese from the neighbouring farm, for instance, has to be a better choice than an organic cheese made elsewhere, packaged and sent here. I find the organic craze a little hard to understand – has it become a status thing?"

(Alastair's note: it is harder to understand in Italy than elsewhere, for Italy has such a long tradition of small producers known and trusted by their community. Organic is, indeed, often the choice of city dwellers, removed as they are from food producers. Certainly it is rare to find such a passion for organic food among country dwellers who are confident in the integrity and competence of their neighbouring farmers. I, though, am nevertheless a stalwart defender of the organic system, knowing something of the grim industry that is most food production.)

Ilaria and Maurizio organise tasting sessions of local produce and of their own honeys, oils and jams. You can buy all these, plus hand-crafted presents and other local produce in the tasting room. The wood from the land around Rocolo, used to fuel their house, is also made into furniture by Maurizio; he makes toys, picture frames and walking sticks, too.

There are animals everywhere. "They are part of the equilibrium of our lives. We all respect them and the children know how to look after them. Our guests can even bring their own animals. We like cooking vegetarian food, even if we do occasionally eat meat." Maurizio ran a restaurant in Verona, and Ilaria has written three cookbooks; so you know the food will be exceptional.

Maurizio bravely restored part of the structure – which dates from 1800 – himself, and the result looks authentic and attractive: big and airy rooms

have simple cotton rugs over stripped bedroom floors, rough and whitewashed plastered walls, solid country furniture and excellent beds and bathrooms. There's also, usefully, a shared kitchen. Breakfast is delicious, with seasonal cakes and home-grown fruits. Conversation usually bubbles.

Plans were underway to install a salt-water pool but were blocked; they had wanted to heat it entirely by solar panels but the number needed were not authorised. "Aesthetics still rule in much of Italy's planning strategy so we can't always make the choices we would like. But we are optimistic that we will realise our plan," says Ilaria.

There is, nearby, a WWF-managed forest and there are nature trails galore on the farm and beyond. It's an easy place to be, even though there is a keen sense of purpose. Join in with it all or simply settle into the quiet that is everywhere.

Ilaria & Maurizio Corazza

Ca' del Rocolo, via Gaspari 3, loc. Quinto, 37142 Verona
- 2 doubles, 1 family room, €60–€75 (€410–€450 per week).
- Snacks available on request, €15.
- +39 045 8700879
- www.cadelrocolo.com
- Train station: Verona Porta Nuova, 12km; Verona Porta Vescovo, 8km.

Agriturismo La Faula

FRIULI-VENEZIA-GIULIA

The story of Luca and Paul's journey at La Faula is worthy of one of the ubiquitous-but-amusing documentaries that appear to be on every television channel. Two successful businessmen are living and working in London and enjoying the metropolitan life. Neither wants a country life but when the call goes up to lend a hand on a farm, the daring duo dash off as full of good intentions as they are devoid of appropriate skills.

Idanna and Franco, Luca's parents, needed to step back from the hard physical work of running a large farm on a hilly site but didn't want to retire completely. The obvious solution was to see if their urbanised son wanted to take over the reins. As soon as the seed of the idea was planted, it blossomed into a reality for Luca and partner Paul. One day they were on the London Underground, commuting to their jobs in law and marketing, and the next they were working on the land learning quite how little they knew about agriculture. "A huge wave broke over us as soon as we arrived. We needed to learn about forestry, viticulture, viniculture, animal husbandry," says Paul. "Suddenly our days were full of tractor-driving, wood-cutting, vine-pruning, delivering calves, digging drains, making wine. At times it was a daunting struggle."

Their tenacity paid dividends, and they have created a modern working farm where rural laissez-faire and the commerce of a serious winemaker happily mingle. As often happens when someone makes a 'discovery' about a corner of the world they barely knew, there is an urge to share the secret. So Paul, now an eloquent evangelist for the area, had the brave idea of opening the house for bed and breakfast. "We realised that our joy could be shared and that there could be a powerful synergy between the

Casa del Grivò

FRIULI-VENEZIA-GIULIA

The smallholding is in a hamlet on the edge of a plain; behind, densely wooded hills extend to the Slovenian border, sometimes crossed just for the gathering of wild berries. From the bedroom balconies there are wonderful views over the treetops; in autumn, the smell of wood-smoke wafts around the chalet, and, with the low sun's long shadows, creates a wonderful, almost alpine, atmosphere.

The task of relaxing here is made easier by the family's palpable happiness. Guests have spoken of the artistic atmosphere and of Toni and Paola's absolute commitment to doing the right thing environmentally, socially and communally.

"The reconstruction has been done largely by ecological methods," says Toni. "We used all the original building materials that we could find around the property, all that had been discarded because they had fallen out of place or were too damaged. We repaired hand-made roof tiles, chestnut beams, floor tiles and hand-carved flagstones. These materials happen to be worth a fortune now but we used them to save them from waste and because they bring with them

a sense of their past life here. They add extra pleasure to the building."

Simplicity, rusticity and a 'green' approach are the keynotes here; so you'll sleep on traditional, and immensely comfortable, wool and vegetable fibre-filled mattresses, some with blankets and some with handsome quilts. Children will adore the open spaces, the ready-made playmates, the animals and the little pool that's been created by diverting a stream. It is a convivial space, shared easily by the family.

Everywhere there are little displays of old tools, antique jugs, pretty plates. "Our guests say that it feels like stepping into a fairytale. There are many old objects, too, as in a museum, but this is a living house, our home, so it is not static and silent."

Toni celebrates traditional farming – growing for yourself and for your community – for the self-sufficiency it gifted. "There was no middle-man and a farmer had independence. Farming then stood for everything that totalitarianism does not."

They delight in each season and the fruits that

CASA DEL GRIVÒ

each gives them. Each crop sets off a spell of conviviality as friends, neighbours and family gather to help harvest and preserve the organic fruits and vegetables. The main crop is grapes and 2009 marks their 20th year of organic farming. Wine from this region is considered by many to be the finest of all Italian wines and Toni and Paola make three.

"Our Tocai Friuban is a dry white, good with prosciutto, the Refosco dal Peduncolo Rosso is a ruby red dry solid wine for meats and intense flavours and Verduzzo, a tasty straw yellow wine, excellent with risotto or strong cheeses," says Toni. There's a touching story behind the labels, which are exquisite, and Toni will tell you if you ask.

> "Days draw gently to a close at Casa del Grivò: fires are lit, tables laid, glasses polished and fine dinners are cooked by Paola"

They point to the Slow philosophy of wine production: an elderly gent holds a rake and with it he is drawing the lines for a musical score. "Producing our wine is like working on a melody," says Toni.

Maps are laid out at breakfast, and there are heaps of books on the region; the walking is wonderful, there are a castle to visit and a river to picnic by. It is an area as rich in art, architecture, monuments and history as any in Italy. To ignore the Friuli would be a great shame, so do add it to the list! It is steeped in fascinating history yet is small enough to be navigated easily by bus, train or bike. A visit to Cividale del Friuli will plunge you into the history of Julius Caesar's arrival in 50BC. It was called Forum Iuli in honour of the Emperor and from those origins came the word Friuli. Market day is lively and you will see influences in the food from Yugoslavia, Slovenia and Austria.

The art collections of Udine are well-known, and the whole area has more than a flavour of Venice. Aquileia has important early Christian history and the basilica shields extensive remains of a Roman port. From its mosaic floor, depicting ocean scenes, soar mighty Corinthian columns. Friulanos are proud of their history and the language of Friuli is enjoying a renaissance: you may even see road signs in Friulano. The Società Filogica Friulana in Udine houses studies on the fraught history of Italy's much-invaded north-eastern corner and has catalogued important developments in the dialect.

Days draw gently to a close at Casa del Grivò: fires are lit, tables laid, glasses polished and fine dinners are cooked by Paola using old recipes and their own and local produce. There is candlelight and wine, too, and maybe even music and singing.

Toni & Paola Costalunga

Casa del Grivò,
Borgo Canal del Ferro 19, 33040 Faédis

- 1 double, 4 family rooms, €60. Half-board €50 p.p.
- Dinner with wine, from €25. Lunch in summer only.
- +39 0432 728638
- www.casadelgrivo.com
- Train station: Udine

B&B Valferrara

EMILIA-ROMAGNA

There is an endearing simplicity to the bones of this Emilia-Romagna tower house, for its personality has been nurtured by Cosetta and Giuliano. They arrived at the 17th-century sandstone Casa a Scale – 'tiered house' – in 1994 and wanted to do nothing more than allow the old ruins to breathe again and reveal their natural beauty.

Nothing has been overdone; all is understated, and fittingly so, in this silent hamlet on the ancient road that once linked Canossa with Carpineti. When it was a travellers' lodge, weary merchants would stop here, absorbing the protective calm of the surrounding forested hills before resuming their journeys to market. There were less benign travellers, too – the *briganti*, or bandits; but it's unlikely that a well-defended *fortezza* such as this would have come under attack. The house survived all sorts of turmoils and sits securely in the Tuscan-Emilian National Park.

Here you can slough off the self-absorption and frenzy of the modern world. There are three bedrooms for guests and an unusual amount of space to inhabit: a red-sofa'd living room and a large log-fired dining area that opens onto the garden. The feeling is of staying as friends, and the gentle hospitality of Cosetta and Giuliano has been praised by many a happy guest.

Cosetta's passion is furniture restoration. The house is full of antiques, gleaming wood, and even a parquet floor made from reclaimed roof timbers. "I always try to work faithfully. I want to be sure, even, that every key and lock is the right one for the age of the house. My greatest pleasure is when guests appreciate it all," she says.

Cosetta's story embraces slow cooking, as it does so often in Italy. She creates jams that most of us would never think of, such as rosemary and fig and experimental berry mixes. She bottles

them, not always to sell but often to give to guests – a typically generous gesture. Her shelves sag under the weight of cookbooks ancient and modern and, thus equipped, she is able to produce wonderful local dishes such as spinach and ricotta wrap with locally ground wheat. "We love inspiring our guests with our recipes and helping them discover the farms that sell produce. In Latteria there is a famous place to buy parmesan and there are many traditional restaurants in the area."

Local produce includes honey and home-grown vegetables from the orto. Her own garden is grassed but it is seemingly without boundaries and tumbles into a prettier, wilder, landscape.

You can see the delicate tower of the Carpineti castle from the house. Nearby Canossa is rich in architectural and historical interest and its own castle, in a strategic position above the Secchia and Enza valleys, is where Emperor Henry IV was made to stand outside in the snow for three days as penance for his interference in the ecclesiastical appointments proposed by Pope Gregory VII.

Cosetta's ambition is to open three little apartments in the grounds so that guests will stay for a week or two and properly explore the area. "We have Slow Food Festivals and can organise walking tours. I plan to hold music events in our own garden, too." She is a gentle helmswoman and imbues the whole place with a sense of family and homeliness that is appreciated by all.

Cosetta Mordacci & Giuliano Beghi

B&B Valferrara,
via Valferrara 14, Pantano, 42033 Carpineti

- 3 doubles, €76–€90.
- Restaurants 1–4km.
- +39 340 1561417
- www.bb-valferrara.it
- Train station: Reggio Emilia

La Piana dei Castagni Agriturismo

EMILIA-ROMAGNA

Roughly etched into a piece of wood leaning against a wall by Piana dei Castagni's front door are these words: "I awake with the scent of the forests wafting in through the open window; I look out and watch the hawks soaring effortlessly through the sky. The smell of freshly baked biscuits floats up the stairs to where I am standing." Valeria's words are simple, home truths. "I'm no poet!" she laughs. "They just come from the heart. Mornings here really are like that!"

And life here couldn't be simpler or more genuine. You won't trip up over any ostentatious gestures; quite the opposite. The tempo is slow, to the point of being almost at a standstill, the mood relaxed. "We want guests to feel that all this is theirs; only then will they really, truly relax."

Valeria's father restored the simple farmhouse nearly 20 years ago. Now she and her husband and young son live a little way away down a tree-lined track which only boosts your sense of blissful, restorative isolation.

Baskets overflowing with geraniums dangle beneath brown-shuttered windows. A pale yellow rose clambers boldly over a window arch, pinning itself to the weathered bricks as it goes. The lovely lawns aren't manicured and are dotted with fallen leaves and shady trees; the garden's boundaries and wild borders beyond are blurred. In fact it's hard to tell where Valeria's land stops and the rest of the valley begins as the uneven, grassy slopes tumble down to the valley below. The whole place seems to thrive on its isolation.

Although historically an agriturismo, Piana dei Castagni doesn't produce its own oil or press its own grapes. Their sense of what is Slow is more subtle, though no less tangible. "It's not the activities that we do which are Slow, it's the way that we live," explains Valerie. "And that has drawn many types of

guests – particularly artists who are drawn to the peace and seclusion and, of course, to the landscape.

"Guests turn up, a pile of books tucked under one arm, and maybe an easel and set of paints under the other, and they're content. They don't need anything else. I'm just happy that I have the space for them so that they can enjoy doing the things they love in such peace."

La Piana is productive in another way. There is something, hidden in the surrounding greenery, that they produce in abundance. "This is the land of the chestnut tree (castagno)!" Valeria claims, proudly. The chestnut trees have been here since medieval times and are as poignant a feature of the landscape of Emilia-Romagna as rows of cypress trees are to her western neighbour, Tuscany. Surrounding the farmhouse is acre upon acre of this ancient woodland. Guests can follow the paths which wriggle their way through the trees, skirting around huge trunks, some of them over 300 years old. "Il pane dei poveri (the bread of the poor)

"When the time's right, in the autumn, we collect the chestnuts then dry them in the kiln"

played an intrinsic nutritional role during the Second World War. At that time everything was made from chestnut flour and polenta; that's all anybody ate!" says Valeria.

The significance of the chestnut tree appears to be as important in local life today as it was then. "When the time's right, in the autumn, we collect the chestnuts then dry them in the kiln. Just before Christmas, we make chestnut flour." The water-mill next to the farmhouse still churns away, grinding up the chestnuts, just as it has been doing for hundreds of years. "These ancient woodlands are so rich in history and tradition. And that's why we protect the castagni, because they have been such an integral part of our livelihood for generations."

Piana dei Castagni's menu has come a long way since the 1940s and Valeria is a wonderful cook. Nowadays you're more likely to come across regional dishes, with the occasional unusual one thrown in, such as Valeria's tortelloni alle ortiche (tortelloni in a nettle sauce). They're all accompanied by vegetables plucked straight from the well-tended garden. "Sometimes we'll all muck in together in the kitchen, my husband, father and son. It's a team effort!"

Plaques on the doors of the simple, snug bedrooms depict fruits of neighbouring forests, with one exception, of course; 'Chestnut' is brighter and more spacious, with wooden floors topped with colourful rugs.

"It's strange to think of us as part of a movement, a Slow movement," Valeria says. "This is just the way we are. But it is rewarding that people appreciate what we do here."

Signora Valeria Vitali

La Piana dei Castagni Agriturismo, via Lusignano 11, 40040 Rocca di Roffeno

- 2 doubles, €60–€90. 2 triples, €80–€100.1 single, €40.
- Dinner €17. Wine €8–€15. Restaurant 3km.
- +39 0519 12985
- www.pianadeicastagni.it
- Train station: Vergato

La Sosta di Ottone III

LIGURIA

At La Sosta, 200 metres above sea level and on a large ridge, the views up and down – and all round – are riveting. Angela and Fabio thoroughly appreciate that they owe much to their local Slow chapter for, as well as communicating the Slow Food philosophy to the broader community, it is a vigilant guardian of the landscape, the culture and even the mood of the town.

"The fact that Levanto is a Slow city, and that we are on the edge of the Cinque Terre National Park, does give a sense of security; it is unlikely that much of what we love about living here will change," says Angela. "We exist in a democracy yet there is a moral onus on those applying for planning permission to respect our environment and to bring something of quality to the area. A five-year planning programme means that all interested parties have a chance to vet proposals and give their opinions."

Fabio, Angela and her mother, Jo, are devoted members of the Slow Food movement. They attend Chapter meetings and have twice heard Carlo Petrini, an inspiring speaker and the movement's founder, talk in Levanto. Naturally, they source the best local food to serve in their own restaurant, but such dedication requires careful planning. "We ask guests to pre-book dinners because we buy what we need for that day. We don't have frozen or pre-made foods and can't suddenly conjure up extra meals for late guests."

Fabio cooks with the help of Fulvia; she is the pastry and puddings expert and he the sommelier. The wine list includes carefully selected Ligurian wines and some regional varieties that are not well-known outside Italy. The restaurant is in the converted cellar and its terrace opens onto a long-reaching view of Chiesanuova, Levanto and the Mediterranean.

The steep hills that tumble down to the jumble of multi-coloured houses on the famous Ligurian Cinque

Terre coastline are dotted with neat allotments, pretty gardens and lines of billowing washing. There is one narrow road through Chiesanuova but cars are not allowed; so enjoy the peace and be prepared to carry your luggage down a footpath to the house.

La Sosta di Ottone ('sosta' means stopover) is named thus for it is said that Otto III stayed here on his way to his coronation in Rome in 996. The listed 16th-century house has been restored with the required reverence, using Ligurian stone and local marble. Bedrooms and bathrooms are exceptionally comfortable and large.

There is great comfort at La Sosta but this is not a hotel. There are spaces to sit and read yet you will not find staff dashing about to cater to your every whim. Sybarites may lament that the

> "My favourite path is the 8B. It overlooks one Cinque Terre town after another with the sea laid out beneath. It is breathtaking"

nearest bar is a 15-minute walk. The comfort of the rooms and the high quality of breakfast and dinner are evidence, though, that behind the scenes wheels are turned energetically on your behalf.

"Guests looking for great walking will be delighted," says Angela. "Several footpaths, some of which lead to the National Park and others to villages in the Levanto valley, cross Chiesanuova. It is 35 minutes to the Levanto beach and 45 on the way back up. One three-hour trail, with only one 15-minute stretch on a road, delivers you to one of the most spectacular parts of the national park. There are many choices of paths, high and low. My favourite path is the 8B. It overlooks one Cinque Terre town after another with the sea laid out beneath. It is breathtaking."

The faint-hearted or less mobile can get around the area with remarkable ease too. Any combination of boat/train/bus can be arranged to get you to and from the five marine hamlets of Monterosso, Vernazza, Corniglia, Manarola and Riomaggiore. Angela, Fabio and daughter Constanza have posted details of lots of walks on their website. They have done them all and have uploaded stacks of photos to inspire you to pack your boots.

Happy are they who have found their corner of paradise before their time is up. To have your corner of paradise within a stone's throw of Levanto, one of Italy's Slow cities, is enough to fill your cup to overflowing. The best part of belonging to a community that is dedicated to all things Slow is that much of what you love will remain unchanged.

Fabio & Angela Graziani

La Sosta di Ottone III,
loc. Chiesanuova 39, 19015 Levanto
- 1 double, 2 family rooms for 2–4, 1 suite for 4, from €180.
- Breakfast €10. Dinner €35. Restaurant 5km.
- +39 0187 814502
- www.lasosta.com
- Train station: Monterosso

[TUSCANY]

TUSCANY

Tuscany, the cradle of the Renaissance, and Florence its capital, are a treasure trove of architectural, painted, and sculpted gems, each one seeming to outshine the other. Its towns – such as Lucca, Pisa, Siena, San Gimignano – are as familiar to us as the names of its sons Michelangelo, Leonardo, Botticelli, Galileo and Dante. So too are the names of the galleries: Uffizi, Accademia, and Bargello. The landscape of undulating hills clad in disciplined rows of vines, blue mountains, cypress trees and medieval hilltop towns peeping through morning mists has been so celebrated by renaissance masters, Oscar-scooping directors and advertising agencies that it is in danger of becoming clichéd. Yet we never tire of Tuscany.

Venus, the mythical goddess of beauty, broke her necklace and its seven pearls dropped into the sea. As they touched the water they turned into a string of islands – the Tuscan archipelago. The largest is L'Isola d'Elba, best-known as Napoleon's place of exile. The second is the tiny Isola di Giglio, a short trip by ferry from Porto Santo Stefano. As the boat approaches the simple little houses that cluster around the port one sees that Il Porto is in fact an animated little town with diminutive sandy beaches. A steep, winding bus journey takes you to the cool and peace of Il Castello, the walled town at the top of the island.

Before the arrival of the Etruscans, Tuscany was inhabited by Apennine peoples. Over the centuries, City States grew and prospered and, by the time the Romans came in the first century, the Etruscans had ceded all power. Lucca, Pisa, Siena and Florence were established; roads, aqueducts, sewers, domestic and public buildings were built.

"blue mountains and hilltop towns peeping through morning mists"

After the fall of Rome, Goths and Longobardi picked up the mantle and there was more building – Vicenza, for example. During the medieval period, pilgrims travelling across the region on their way from France to Rome brought huge wealth to the area and new communities grew up around churches and inns.

The conflict between Guelphs and Ghibellines split the Tuscan people but increased the wealth of communes such as Arezzo, Florence, Lucca, Pisa and Siena. Florence became the renaissance capital, Pisa its port (it was once on the sea), Siena and Lucca centres of finance.

The Medici family ruled Florence in the 15th century and annexed the surrounding lands to create modern-day Tuscany. In the 18th century the Duke of Lorraine took over from the Medicis and Florence became part of the Holy Roman Empire. This was later dissolved by Napoleon and became part of the Austrian Empire until it was transferred to the newly unified nation of Italy. (Austrian troops had even occupied Venice, much to the disgust of the proud Venetians.)

Tuscany has vast swathes of lush forest and woodland of beech, chestnut and oak. From September to January you can join the Tuscans in their passion for hunting and foraging. In season you may find mushrooms, truffles, chestnuts and berries, or just walk and savour the sounds, scents and beauty.

In the gentle hills of Val d'Arbia there is a network of 67 tracks for walking, biking and riding; take the medieval pilgrim's way along the Via Francigena; follow a route connecting historic fortifications or discover Etruscan ruins and tombs along the Valle dell'Ombrone.

Many Tuscan villages are famous for their crafts: Scarperia is the town of knives and its charter for apprentices and master craftsmen was drawn up in the 16th century. You can watch a horn-handled knife being fashioned in one of the little knife shops. Other villages produce goods crafted from leather, wood or alabaster. Impruneta is well known for its clay quarries and terracotta furnaces, some of which date back to the 16th century and are still used to fire fine terracotta pots.

Massa Marittima is a fascinating hill town with distant views to the sea at Follonica; a puzzle of tiny streets and staunch palazzi. The colourful Torneo della Balestra (crossbow) is enacted in costume. In the evening young lovers, silver-haired gents, mothers and small sons dance together to the booming sounds of the town's brass band.

The fashionable coastal towns of Punta Ala and Castiglione della Pescaia are choc-a-block in August. Further north is Viareggio – home to the most flamboyant of all Italian carnivals.

Arezzo hosts a summer Polifonica music festival and Cortona the Tuscan Sun Festival of classical music, renaissance art, food, literature.

Each Italian region has its own dialect but the 12th-century literary language of Florence and of its sons Dante, Petrarca and Boccaccio, was the basis of the Italian language and Florentines maintain they speak the purest, most sophisticated Italian.

Lindy Wildsmith

TUSCANY

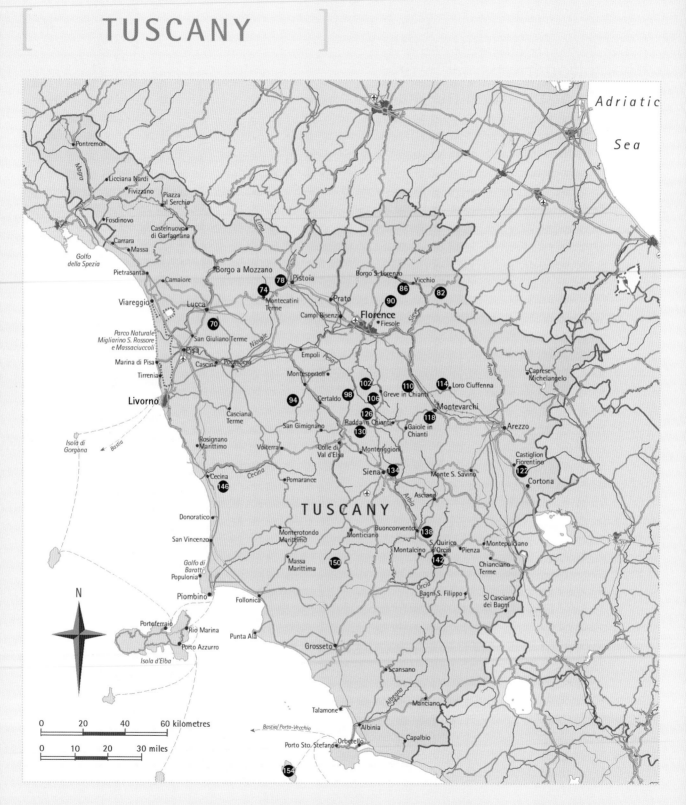

Adriatic

Sea

Pontremoli

Licciana Nardi

Fivizzano

Piazza
al Serchio

Fosdinovo

Carrara

Massa

*Golfo
della Spezia*

Pietrasanta

Camaiore

Castelnuovo
di Garfagnana

Borgo a Mozzano

Viareggio

Lucca

Montecatini
Terme

78 Pistoia

Prato

Borgo S. Lorenzo

Vicchio

86

82

90

74

Campi Bisenzio

Florence

Fiesole

70

San Giuliano Terme

Marina di Pisa

Pisa

Cascina

Pontedera

Empoli

Tirrenia

Livorno

*Isola di
Gorgona*

Bastia

*Parco Naturale
Migliarino S. Rossore
e Massaciuccoli*

Montespertoli

102

110

114 Loro Ciuffenna

*Caprese
Michelangelo*

Certaldo **98**

106

Greve in Chianti

94

Casciana
Terme

San Gimignano

126

Radda in Chianti

Montevarchi

118

Gaiole in
Chianti

Arezzo

Rosignano
Marittimo

Volterra

130

Colle di
Val d'Elsa

Montereggioni

Castiglion
Fiorentino

122

Cortona

Cecina

Pomarance

Siena **134**

Monte S. Savino

146

Donoratico

TUSCANY

Asciano

San Vincenzo

Monterotondo
Marittimo

Monticiano

Buonconvento

138

S. Quirico
d'Orcia

Pienza

Montepulciano

Montalcino

*Golfo di
Baratti*
Populonia

Massa
Marittima

150

142

Chianciano
Terme

Piombino

Follonica

Bagni S. Filippo

S. Casciano
dei Bagni

Portoferraio

Rio Marina

Punta Ala

Grosseto

Scansano

Manciano

Porto Azzurro

Isola d'Elba

Talamone

Capalbio

Bastia/Porto-Vecchio

Albinia

154

Porto Sto. Stefano

Orbetello

N

0   20   40   60 kilometres

0   10   20   30 miles

Special places to stay

Tuscany

70 Villa Michaela

74 Antica Casa 'Le Rondini'

78 Tenuta di Pieve a Celle

82 Le Due Volpi

86 Villa Campestri

90 Casa Palmira

94 Fattoria Barbialla Nuova

98 Sovigliano

102 Azienda Agricola Il Borghetto

106 Fattoria Viticcio Agriturismo

110 Locanda Casanuova

114 Odina Agriturismo

118 Agriturismo Rendola Riding

122 Relais San Pietro in Polvano

126 La Locanda

130 Fattoria Tregole

134 Frances' Lodge

138 Podere Salicotto

142 Il Rigo

146 Podere Le Mezzelune

150 Pieve di Caminino

154 Il Pardini's Hermitage

Villa Michaela

TUSCANY

Just ten minutes from the beautiful city of Lucca. To get here you follow a tiny road called Via di Valle which takes you past the Vorno church and winds up the hill, through olive groves and onto the mountain where it becomes a track and finally peters out. So there is little traffic and all you hear is the whisper of the breeze and the occasional chiming of the church bells.

Tuscany does it again – another eye-popping house looking over a vast range of hills and forests, in this case 50 acres of pine with the olive groves beyond. Here you also have a fine garden, heady with gardenias, plus a tennis court and a pool. There is more than a touch of opulence too, something often found with foreign owners driven by the magic of Tuscany. The grander bedrooms have frescoed ceilings, lavish fabrics, huge beds and double sinks. Puccini, Verdi and Dante are the names of those rooms, and you may well find yourselves listening to opera music while you float around in a haze of admiration.

Vanessa bought the villa in 1984 when it was a comparatively simple structure. "It was a bit like a grand

country barn and, like many of the houses up here, it was the second home of a Lucchese family. These old villas were traditionally used for little more than six to eight weeks in summer when their owners would flee the heat of the city and take off to the hills in their horse and carriage."

The renovation was a project on a grand scale – taking it on today would be even more challenging.

"Commendably the Italian government has put in place stringent regulations to ensure buildings are energy efficient," says Vanessa. "We have converted an outbuilding and we must install solar panels and rainwater reservoirs. We embrace the measures.

"We have a heat-exchange system for the pool and the air-conditioning and use long-life bulbs everywhere. We ask guests to be mindful of water usage. The English take it well but some others have an 'I have paid and I will indulge myself' attitude. They think we are simply trying to save money so I need to present a more scientific argument to persuade all to join in happily!

"Recycling collections are efficient and regular. We aim

to constantly reduce our waste; we buy fresh
stuff at markets and buy in bulk. In England
I can't believe the waste created by supermarket
packaging.

"We are enthusiastic supporters of Vorno's
wonderful village store run by Alba; she sells fresh
produce that she buys from local people and is
something of an institution locally. We buy our
breakfast croissants there."

Scallop Risotto
Serves 6

1kg (2lb) scallops, shelled and cleaned
125g (4oz) butter
4 tablespoons brandy
sea salt and freshly ground pepper
3 shallots, finely chopped
500g (1lb) Carnaroli rice
1.5 litres (3 pints) hot fish stock
2 tablespoons flat leaf parsley, finely chopped
3 tablespoons double cream

• Separate corals from scallops
• Heat half the butter and sauté the scallops for 2-3
minutes, turning once
• Pour on brandy and ignite it. Season when flames
die down, and put to one side
• Sauté shallots in remaining butter until soft
• Add rice and mix. Heat until the rice is crackling hot
and shiny
• Pour in a ladleful of hot stock. Stir and let the
grains absorb the liquid. Repeat until the rice is
almost cooked
• Add the scallops, corals, juices and parsley. Stir and
resume the cooking process as before
• Take off heat when rice is creamy and velvety but
has a slight bite. Stir in the cream and cover
• Leave to rest for 2 minutes. Spoon onto a warmed
platter. Serve at once with chilled white wine and
rocket salad

Vanessa has organised Slow Food house-parties by liaising with the Slow Food Movement's Presidia in Tuscany. For instance, for one event they gathered together little-known cheeses for tastings from one of Tuscany's forgotten areas – the north-western corner within which lies the alpine-like Garfagnana National Park.

Vanessa is at the villa for six months of the year. In her absence Robert and Massimo take care of guests. Massimo is an architect and art historian and has stacks of knowledge that he is happy to share so you are in intelligent hands.

Vorno is famous for its spring – people arrive with empty bottles to fill up and take home. It is collected each day for the villa's guests, too.

You can get here easily: train to Lucca, hourly bus to Vorno and then five minutes of walking to the house. To get your fix of medieval Tuscany you need only drop down into Lucca. There you can cycle around the entirely intact city walls and take in a concert; this is Puccini's birthplace and the city is alive with music.

If you are assailed by delusions of grandeur during your stay at Villa Michaela you can hire two sopranos and a tenor to sing to you in the garden. This is more of a palazzo than a villa, and the mountain belongs to it – as does the chapel, so you could even marry here.

Vanessa Swarbreck

Villa Michaela,
via di Valle 8, 55060 Vorno

- 10 doubles, €200–€300. Entire villa on request.
- Dinner with wine, €50.
- +44 (0)7768 645500
- www.villamichaela.com
- Train station: Lucca

Antica Casa 'Le Rondini'

TUSCANY

Expectations soar on the approach to Antica Casa. The village of Colle di Buggiano is resolutely medieval: narrow cobbled streets, towering church towers, a tiny village square where elderly ladies sit in the shade playing cards for money, dogs lie in the sun and the church clock solemnly declares the time. The scene is so exquisitely set for something magnificent that you might wonder if your chosen place to stay could possibly measure up and keep the fairytale alive.

Antica Casa exceeds expectations. Imagine a room above an archway within the castle walls of this ancient hilltop village, a room with 200-year-old frescoes depicting swallows swooping and diving and where, when you lean out from the window, you realise it is all for real as the swallows (rondini) flit in and out of nests in the archway.

Embracing Slow can mean many things; here

it is celebrated in Carlo's determination to restore and renovate the shell of the 500-year-old house that they found nine years ago. As an architect he had the credentials to do the job creatively and knowledgeably; he is Vice President of Bio-Architecture at Pistoia University. "We travelled widely," says Fulvia, "and when we first returned to Italy I taught PE and martial arts at a school in Venice. When we adopted a six-year-old boy from Russia, Federico, we decided upon the move to Tuscany. It was so important to us to find something special. We found this house, which has foundations dating from 900, in a state of abandonment. It was far too big, but we fell in love with it and refused to be deterred!"

It is impossible to resist. The combined charms of the house, the garden, the owners, the nearby hilltop restaurant with memorable views – they vanquish you. "One lady was in tears when she told

me that we had the house that she had dreamed of. I do feel proud and lucky," says Fulvia.

An archway off the Via del Vento ('where the wind blows') leads to the house. You step into a lovely room, a study in white – fresh lilies and snowy walls and sofas – dotted with family antiques and paintings; everywhere there is elegance. Delightfully different bedrooms have wrought-iron bedheads, big mirrors, thick padded eiderdowns, daybeds, pretty headboards; the suite is especially attractive.

The garden, opposite, was nurtured as gently as the house and was created from the plot of an ancient derelict property. It is now alive with lemon trees, flowers and scented herbs, a sensuous place to which Fulvia takes breakfast for guests. It is an oasis in the middle of the village. The hillsides beneath scramble down to the Montecatini Terme plains and are tinged with the silver of olive trees. Such is the architectural significance of this village and many of its buildings that Carlo has been unable to introduce many of the ecological innovations used in his professional projects. "There are many rules and regulations that apply because of the age of the house. We can't have solar panels, for example. We are making small changes where we can, though, and have managed to harvest rainwater from the roofs into an ancient central cistern."

Their restoration has been a nine-year journey – "a demanding one," says Fulvia, "but one that has brought us happiness and great satisfaction."

Fulvia Musso

Antica Casa 'Le Rondini',
via M Pierucci 21, 51011 Colle di Buggiano

* 5 doubles, €75–€115. Apartment for 2-4, €65 for 2.
* Restaurant 200m.
* +39 0572 33313
* www.anticacasa.it
* Train station: Montecatini Terme

Tenuta di Pieve a Celle

TUSCANY

Unity is a leitmotif running through Pieve a Celle, something that Fiorenza Saccenti values above most things: the unity of guests and family, of conversation and conviviality, of their life and the life of the community.

The Saccentis – three generations of them – live at the ochre 'colonica' at the end of the cypress tree-lined drive. For them Pieve a Celle is an island, a paradise – albeit a hardworking one. They run it in a delightful spirit of inclusivity, encouraging others to join in with the rhythms of their family life. "We have our own perfect ecosystem and are lucky enough to be able to produce our own organic olive oil, wine and vegetables. We appreciate, too, being in a part of the world where respect is given to tradition, to local food and to artisan producers."

Fiorenza does something that we can all do, wherever we live, and that is focus on the little things that make us happy. If we fall into the trap of seeing happiness as a big goal to achieve, we miss out on an easily-achievable sense of contentment

"I have a deep love of small pleasures for they bring

me the greatest happiness. It is something sweet taken from the oven and filling the room with a beautiful smell, a good coffee poured for friends, flowers from the garden on the kitchen table, even the dog wagging its tail!" And these are the things that can bring happiness to us all, slow though we may often be to recognise it. We need, perhaps, to give ourselves enough time to celebrate our fortune.

(It is in celebration of small pleasures that the community of Findhorn in Scotland has had such a remarkable success over many years, for it was founded on the notion of there being 'gods of small things' – the 'divas' which they saw in their vegetables. Mocked they were, of course, but so mighty were their vegetables that people all over the world acknowledged a truth, and came.)

"We have had many wonderful times with guests, sitting on the terrace under summer skies and stars, or around a fire in winter, sharing some good wine. These are the things that people appreciate and savour when they are on holiday with us."

Among the many fine things here – the beautiful fabrics

designed by Cesare, the family antiques, the luxuries
that give deep comfort to your stay such as lovely
bathrooms and beds – the practical things that
make the farm work are respected, almost revered.
"The olive mill, for example, is very important. Every
year for many years people have gathered around it,
tended it, and appreciated the conviviality of
working with it at harvest time."

The house reflects the warmth and elegance of
its owners. There are cabinets with pretty china,
hand-printed bedspreads and curtains, African art,

> "I have a deep love of small
> pleasures; these bring me the
> greatest happiness. It is
> something sweet taken from the
> oven and filling the room with a
> beautiful smell, a good coffee
> poured for friends, flowers from
> the garden"

antique rugs on terracotta floors. Bedrooms are
pretty and undeniably Italian in style; one has its
own private entrance from the patio.

Cesare and Fiorenza share a deep love of art and
music. Cesare studied art and archaeology and has
his own workshops in Prato producing fabric for
clothing. Together they have chosen sculptures,
pictures, and bronzes for the house and garden; the
previous owner was a sculptor and his work is
displayed in the grounds.

This patch of northern Tuscany has saved its
charm from the ravages of modern times. There are
beautiful, medieval working cities with markets and
fine food shops. These tightly built communities
were at the centre of the Renaissance. Many throb
with musical life and festivals. The vitality of Italian
cities feels like something we should be attempting
to reproduce all over the world.

The charms of Pieve a Celle are considerable. The pool – immaculate and with panoramic views from many metres above sea level – is delightful, and handsome with its decking. Lawns, hedges, olive groves and vineyards stretch out in all directions. "We find that people who appreciate our way of life are attracted to stay here," says Fiorenza. "They, like us, enjoy the sense of being in a working community with people who have greater aspirations than simply earning money in the city. It's an organic way of life."

Fiorenza spends much of her time, happily so, in the family kitchen. She makes bread in a wood-fired oven, does imaginative things with veg from the kitchen garden, and with mushrooms foraged from their ten-acre woodland. She makes jams and fruit puddings when the 17 acres have been particularly productive. Dinners are important celebrations, all of them, and have a light-heartedness that is so Italian. They serve their own wine made from Sangiovese grapes. "We don't make lots of wine but enough to share with friends, family and guests. Our oil is sold to local restaurants.

"When we found this house we wanted to make a Slow life here and have embraced the whole philosophy of the movement." One happy guest wrote: "I have never experienced a property more beautiful, a family more genuinely friendly or food more beautifully prepared."

This is praise indeed – and it is richly deserved.

Cesare & Fiorenza Saccenti

Tenuta di Pieve a Celle,
via di Pieve a Celle 158, 51030 Pistoia

- 5 twins/doubles, €120–€140.
- Dinner €30, by arrangement. Wine €8.50–€10.
- +39 0573 913087
- www.tenutadipieveacelle.it
- Train station: Pistoia

Le Due Volpi

TUSCANY

From your eyrie in the Mugello, in this northern corner of Tuscany, it's a short tumble down the hills to the art-soaked cities of Florence, Siena and Arezzo. But once you are here your focus may shift; there is more to Tuscany than art.

"People retreat into the peace and the shade of our garden, away from the crowds," says Heidi Flores. "We are far from a main road and, most importantly, Lorenzo and I don't rush about or live by the clock. We work with ease and I am sure this sense of ease transfers itself to guests."

Instead of sightseeing you may want to walk in the hills, on routes marked out by the Italian Alpine Club, take a short trip to Lake Bilancino, do yoga or have a massage. There is a tangible sense of contentment and playfulness around Heidi and Lorenzo. In a rather typical Slow story they ditched demanding careers and city life for something more satisfying. "I became ill in 2005 and looked hard at my lifestyle," says Heidi. "I was an education administrator, at the beck and call of too many people. Friends pointed out that making a change might be a good idea and we landed here in 2006.

"I have never looked back. This house was a cure. I have become a different person!" Their enthusiasm for guests is very real and they are genuinely happy for you to linger all day. "There is space enough for everyone to be undisturbed. Time has less significance here," says Heidi, "and seeing guests unwind is rewarding for us."

Lorenzo owns a *cantina* in Fiesole in the hills above Florence, a shop where you can buy the wines and delicacies of Tuscany. He shares his knowledge with all those wanting to learn more about Italian wine and can arrange tastings, too. As a young man his passion was cycling; he was an all-Italy champion and his lycra shirt is framed and

hung just near the breakfast room. His hobby is renovating antique radios and gramophones; from his little workshop in the garden may drift the sound of a Neapolitan folk song. The names given to the bedrooms are his favourite models of radios!

Heidi is a polyglot and true cosmopolitan with a particular passion for England. Her large kitchen has been built around a handsome four-oven Aga. It arrived from England in pieces and took the ever-patient Lorenzo two days to assemble.

The bedrooms are pretty, thanks to the English country-house feel. Windows give onto the oak and chestnut woods above and the valley below. Further seduction may come from a massage in a therapy space below the house with windows that give onto panoramic views. The sunny slopes are perfect for the solar panels installed as part of their growing campaign to become more eco-friendly.

Snowy, the Westie, and Heidi will take you to collect eggs from neighbour Silvano. He stores them in his cellar, richly filled with flagons of wine and legs of ham and salami.

Lorenzo will tell you tales of the *sagres* held in local fields. Sagres revolve around a seasonal product, maybe the new wine, the first chestnuts or truffles. The closest English equivalent to these Tuscan fairs is the village fête, though a sagre is far more rumbustious; eating, dancing, drinking and energetic partying are encouraged.

Come in early October and help Silvano during the *vendemmia* (grape harvest) or for Canta Maggio, when folk singers and musicians roam from village to village: they sing to the locals and the villagers offer cheese, salami and a glass of wine. Heidi and Lorenzo have asked them to make Le Due Volpi one of their stop-off points. So May is a good time to visit if you'd like to join in.

Twice a week Heidi and Lorenzo cook for guests. At a communal table under the pergola you can try her panzanella and salads, Lorenzo's Florentine steaks and Silvano's wine – bottled by Lorenzo.

Lorenzo describes these evenings as "a night with the Etruscans"; he is keen to point out that modern Tuscans are upholding the party spirit of their famously feasting, drinking, Etruscan ancestors. Their jollity was celebrated by D H Lawrence in *Etruscan Places* – he derided the empire-building Romans, who "crushed the free soul in people after people".

Heidi runs cookery courses, too; she'll collect you from the train, take you to markets, share her recipes and then create a party atmosphere in which to celebrate the bounty of Tuscany. Is it possible to resist?

Heidi Flores & Lorenzo Balloni

Le Due Volpi,
via di Molezzano 88, 50039 Vicchio del Mugello
- 3 doubles (one with kitchenette), €75–€95.
  Extra bed €20–€30. Half-board option.
- Dinner €25, with local wine. Picnic, with wine, €15.
- +39 055 840 7874
- www.leduevolpi.it
- Train station: Vicchio

Villa Campestri

TUSCANY

Once upon a time in Tuscany olive oil was worth more by weight than the choicest cuts of beef or veal. Then, virtually all oil was of the finest quality. Now that it is a staple foodstuff, prices have tumbled, but so has quality.

At Villa Campestri the olive is revered, even by Italian standards. There is an 'Oleoteca' in the old cellars, cooled by spring water, where you can attend a course on all aspects of the oil: historical, cultural, scientific and gastronomic. Inaugurated in 2002, it was Italy's first to be devoted to olive oil in such a wide-ranging way.

The Pasqualis – father Paolo and daughters Viola and Gemma – run the estate together. Paolo takes charge of the tastings.

"An important part of our oil tasting is to educate people about the right methods of production," says Gemma. "Olives must be crushed within 24 hours of harvest to ensure they are not oxidised. If oxygen enters during the processing, the oil, when ingested, will produce free radicals in the body that result in tissue damage.

"It is frightening that a lot of oil sold in Italy is not even from Italy – olives are simply shipped here to be processed. Many of them are old and have been harvested carelessly."

Gemma can speak with authority: she studied agricultural engineering and gained a PhD in bio-technology at the University of Florence; molecular biology is her speciality. One part of her role at Campestri is to source the best type of trees for the micro-climate. "We are 450 metres above sea level and winters are slightly colder than most tree types like, so we choose carefully."

Their oil is widely used in their restaurant – there is even an 'olive oil menu' that includes chocolate soufflé.

Although Campestri is large, with its 25 rooms, it succeeds in behaving like a private villa. There is little about it, in fact, that is like a hotel. It has a warm, homely mood, with charm and delightful staff to provide it.

Viola looks after guests. She is a genuinely nice woman, softly spoken and very much there for you. The family bought the villa in 1989 and restored it using local architects and appropriate, original materials. They opened it as a hotel in 1991.

Most rooms are in the villa itself, others are across the courtyard in the old farmhouse and dairy where they used to make cheese and butter.

The oldest part of the villa was built in the 13th century and was once the property of the Roti Michelozzi family, who lived there for 700 years. It is said that they commissioned one of Giotto's pupils, Lorenzo Bicci, to fresco the tabernacle at the entrance to the villa. At the same period a chapel was built, and is still consecrated. The frescoes from the 1600s are still there, discovered under the plaster and now revealed. They are superb, and only slightly faded in parts. Inside the house there is a well, too, still there after 600 years. It meant, of course, that they never had to go outside the villa in the cold to get their water.

Although much has changed inside, there still remain wonderful wooden ceilings, terracotta floors, coats of arms, and some wonderful art-deco window panes created in the early 20th century by Galileo Chini. They are still much admired today.

The bedrooms, in Renaissance style, are wonderful – and ineffably comfortable. On each floor there is a big sitting room for your use, with antique furniture, rugs, old fireplaces and massive beams. Each one is charming and invites frequent use. Some of the higher rooms are vaulted with old red brick; bathrooms are beyond criticism.

Breakfast is served in a magnificent room with huge Murano glass chandeliers. You won't, now, be surprised to be offered eggs and bacon with your home-made cakes, fruit and yoghurt. The food is memorable, generous and superb value.

There are 140 hectares of land in which you can wander, land rich with fauna and flora, ancient olive trees, wild cherries and maples. The cypress-lined avenue and fine green lawns set the grand Tuscan tone, as does the big swimming pool with its views over the Mugello Valley and the Chianti Rufina hills.

Gemma is pleased she returned to the Villa with her own family. "In my twenties I wanted to discover the world. In my thirties I realised the best place is home. Here I can combine work with motherhood with ease. We each have our roles and responsibilities and work very well as a team."

Viola Pasquali

Villa Campestri,
via di Campestri 19/22, 50039 Vicchio di Mugello
- 10 doubles, 3 triples, 1 single, 2 suites, 5 junior suites, 4 apartments. €120–€310.
- Dinner €52.
- +39 0558 490107
- www.villacampestri.com
- Train station: Vicchio

Casa Palmira

TUSCANY

It is easy to think of Tuscany as a golden land where everything just appears on a plate: dreaming villas on hillsides washed by the sun, with hardly an effort in sight. *Under the Tuscan Sun*, the American tale of a rich woman settling into Tuscany with the help of an amusing gang of Polish builders, merely made us think that there are always others to do the work. Most of us don't think DIY when we think Fiesole. But Stefano and Assunta are a reminder that this is a land of grit and sweat too. They couldn't afford to hire help to restore the house, so they did it themselves – over ten years. Hence the passion in every brick, their obvious delight in showing it to visitors. They still do everything themselves. Stefano seems capable of making anything the house needs, and more. He uses local wood for furniture, and they have even made their own rugs. Ask – and he will show you how it was done. They grow their vegetables for meals, take guests for walks or bike rides, run cookery classes and churn out huge quantities of pasta and pizza with the help of their students and their wood-fired oven.

It is inevitable that a book on 'Slow' will discuss local food production at length, but these folk are genuinely excited by the production virtues of their region. The cookery classes are offered once a week, so you can take something home with you. They are especially proud of the local flour, made in a mill that still uses the old mill-stone.

The farm is medieval, and beautiful. When the couple arrived in Tuscany in 1985 they met Signora Palmira, the farmer who had spent her life in this house. She led a tranquil and self-sufficient existence. Inspired by the serenity, Assunta and Stefano bought the farm's barn and began to renovate it. They lived next to Signora Palmira for

15 years until she died. Much has changed since then "but," says Assunta, "we hope that people feel her spirit is an enduring presence."

Fiesole is up on the hill above Florence; numerous celebrities and literary people have lived,

> "They do everything themselves. Stefano seems capable of making anything the house needs, and more"

and live, up here. It is only half an hour from Florence's bustle, with superb views on the drive up. Not to explore the countryside on a bike, or on foot, would be a shame. Stefano will ferry you about in his van, taking you to the start of your walk or ride, and Assunta will prepare a picnic basket for you. Irresistible, and in just one and a half hours you can be in Fiesole after walking through the woods. There is no need for a car here.

The rooms are charming: a log-fired sitting room setting the tone, and bedrooms opening off a landing with a brick-walled little garden in the centre, created by Stefano. Two rooms have four-poster beds dressed in Florentine fabrics; all have polished wooden floors.

Casa Palmira is imbued with a sense of substantiality and sustainability. It comes from the considerable skill and love poured into it by its gifted and visionary guardians.

Assunta & Stefano Fiorini-Mattioli

Casa Palmira,
via Faentina 4/1,loc. Feriolo, Polcanto,
50030 Borgo San Lorenzo
• 7 rooms, €85–€110. Apartment for 3-4, €95–€120.
• Dinner with wine, €30. Restaurant 700m.
• +39 0558 409749
• www.casapalmira.it
• Train station: Caldine, 6km

Fattoria Barbialla Nuova

TUSCANY

If you spend your working life and your spare time in contact with nature you are almost bound to have a streak of authenticity running through all you do. There are many modern thinkers who believe that the answer to many of our greatest man-made problems is to re-connect with nature distinctly not man-made. Only thus will we re-learn how to live, how to adopt healthy rhythms, how to co-exist with the complex and inter-dependent world around us, how to see beauty.

The poetry of earth is
never dead;
When all the birds are faint
with the hot sun,
And hide in cooling trees,
a voice will run
From hedge to hedge about
the new-mown mead.

Keats

Guido Manfredi Rasponi, who manages the rugged 500-hectare organic Fattoria Barbialla Nuova with Gianluca, explains: "A Slow way of life can't be forced – if people are not utterly committed it shows. We are Slow through and through: we wait for just the

right moment to collect truffles, we raise our cattle in a leisurely way, giving them all the time they need to grow naturally. We run our agriturismo in a way that we feel helps our guests to leave behind the stresses of life in the modern rat race."

He speaks with burning passion and commitment and goes so far as to decry some of the hundreds of agriturismi that have sprung up all over Italy. "Many of these farms only have one small line of produce and concentrate almost entirely on accommodation. We have olive oil, grains, hay, honey, white truffles, chickens and cattle."

The farm, in a nature reserve, is carved out from a larger estate that was left to Guido; the land has been organic since the early 90s and is perfect for grazing their prized, almost biblical, white Chianine cattle. Raising this breed has been a labour of love for there is double certification involved – one for rare-breed status and another for organic.

They have a little shop on the estate, managed by Sabali, that sells the fruits of their labours – bottles of golden oils, precious preserved white truffles, beef – so that guests can take a flavour of the place home with them. Guido and Gianluca have worked hard to provide somewhere beautiful to stay, even if they themselves still have to keep working hard while you loaf about!

They didn't want to create an agricultural fantasy but wanted to keep their rooms genuinely rustic; they shunned anything showy or ostentatious. "English people particularly appreciate the simplicity of our rooms; they like the spaces and the colours and prefer that they are not out of keeping with the work of the farm or with nature," says Guido.

There are three self-catering farmhouses dotted around the estate, all with sweeping views, all on the top of a hill; 'Le Trosce', with four fireplaces, has several levels but is all open-plan. The three 'Doderi' apartments, embraced by an olive grove, are minimalist; Gianluca's joyous bedcovers and 60s-style furniture in Tuscan colours

"A Slow way of life can't be forced – if people are not utterly committed it shows"

add style, originality and colour. The apartments in 'Brentina', a casa colonica (traditional farmhouse), deeper in the woods, are a touch more primitive, though many will love the simplicity of the whitewashed walls and the handmade staircase; all have delightful bathrooms. Outside are pergolas, patios and pools, cheerful with deckchairs and decking; there are also orchard and hens.

It is a place for the independent, but the pair are always around to help if you need anything. There will be space soon for cooking courses but meanwhile you can invite the resident chef, Lucia, to your apartment for personal tuition, or just sit

back with an aperitif while he works his special magic with an abundance of local produce.

Come in autumn and you will follow in the footsteps of the staff from London's River Café restaurant. They come here annually to hunt for truffles and to keep their restaurant in truffle oil and shavings for the year. Up to 15 kilograms of truffles can be found in one year. The largest found here weighed 300 grams; the biggest ever recorded was a whopping one kilogram (and that would be valued at over £25,000!).

"Imperio is our truffle hunter and he has 40 years of experience," says Guido. "He manages the land year-round and controls the growth of the grey poplars which are rooted in volcanic tufa rock. These poplars are the only trees under which the truffles grow and Imperio knows the best spots to dig. His dog, Toby, seeks them out and many Italians now use dogs rather than the traditional pigs for they are trainable."

So a stay in October or November will bring you closer to the rhythms of nature in this part of Tuscany; the woods yield porcini mushrooms, too, and all around there are autumn berries. Stay in spring and you can join in wildlife walks or take off on your own with special route maps.

The Fattoria is a richly interesting place to stay, run with such verve by young owners who cleverly manage to maintain the best of traditional farming values while wholly embracing the most modern ideas about the future of agriculture. They do it all with panache.

Àrghilo Società Agricola

Fattoria Barbialla Nuova,
via Castastrada 49, 50050 Montaione
• 7 apartments: 2 for 2, 3 for 4, 2 for 6. €420–€1,320. Farmhouse for 8, €1,250–€2,000. Prices per week.
• Self-catering. Restaurant 3km.
• +39 0571 677004/0571 677259
• www.barbiallanuova.it
• Train station: Fucecchio S. Miniato

Sovigliano

TUSCANY

"Our daily life is serene, guided by the rhythms of nature, and not a single day is like another. Each is full of the symbolism of nature and its extraordinary richness, its colours and smells. We lead a life that weaves the past with the present, tradition with innovation." That is Signor Bicego speaking. How many of us wish we could say the same of our own lives?!

The story of Sovigliano started 27 years ago when a young family from the Vento, Claudio, Patrizia and their three children, began the search for a different existence. The ancient farmhouse was alluring enough; the pure air, the hills, the views, the light finished the process of seduction. "We had moved from the city and of course we wondered if it would suit us. Now we believe that anybody who finds what we have here would give in to the charms of the countryside."

They came with a huge respect for the history and tradition of the place – its distinctiveness – but wanted, too, as any young family would, to create their own story. They have done so with respect for the architecture, the locals and the landscape.

Claudia, their daughter, has remained at Sovigliano to help her parents; her two brothers work in Paris and Florence. "She is the future of Sovigliano," says Claudio proudly.

It is a very special place, halfway between Florence and Siena: a pretty loggia opens onto distant views of San Gimignano, barbecues are held by candlelight, B&B and self-catering guests seem equally happy; the latter have a delightfully rustic kitchen to share. One guest wrote to tell us that they had gone to a 'village night' in Tavarnelle, nearby – a convivial occasion where you gather with locals, choose

your own steak and wine from the village shop and watch while your meat is cooked on a communal fire.

Sovigliano is a productive estate. Correggiolo, Frantoio and Leccino are the olive species that the family have cultivated to produce their exceptionally good extra virgin oil. These trees thrive in exposed southern hill sites – the parts of the land here which straddle the Pesa and d'Elso valleys and where the soil is clay-based. They collect the olives by hand and use traditional pressing methods to extract the oil. When first bottled, the oil is a light, vibrant green and then it matures to a deep buttery yellow. It is fragrant and fruity and afficionadoes like to taste it as they would a wine – straight

"We lead a life that weaves the past with the present, tradition with innovation"

from a little glass – or sometimes by dipping in a piece of bread.

They produce their own wine, too, and the Sangiovese red grape thrives on the soil. The harvest is done by hand, and the grape juice is transferred to steel vats before being poured into wooden oak barrels to mature. "We do a lot of it ourselves," says Claudio, "but for the bottling we call in a specialist. The conditions have to be perfect." The wine varies from ruby to crimson to garnet according to the climate and growing conditions. It's a robust companion for roast meat and game, cheese and grilled meat.

"We make grappa too, of course – what else do you expect from a family from the Veneto?" smiles Claudio. "It's made here from our grapes and we add walnuts – picked, according to tradition, on San Giovanni's day when they are still unripe – which are macerated in the grappa for a few

months. It is sweet and fragrant, delicate with a soft touch on the palate."

They work with what the land is happy to give them – sometimes a lot, sometimes less, but always quality is prized over quantity. Some of what they produce is sold here at the farm and guests are encouraged to learn about their family recipes and their Venetian and Tuscan cooking. They can then try their hand at bringing together a meal of entirely local produce in the wonderful large kitchen that is set aside for those who self-cater.

There is much to engage any traveller and Patrizia enthusiastically gathers information for guests on local music festivals and exhibitions.

"Next year will be the 20th anniversary of our belonging here and we hope to celebrate with as many guests as possible. We have grown older but our spirits remain young and our values and philosophy are unchanged."

Signora Patrizia Bicego

Sovigliano,
Strada Magliano 9, 50028 Tavarnelle Val di Pesa
- 2 doubles, 2 twins. €130–€160.
  4 apartments for 2-4, €150–€390.
- Dinner with wine, €35.
- +39 0558 076217
- www.sovigliano.com
- Train station: Florence

Azienda Agricola Il Borghetto

TUSCANY

Can the English make good wine? Well, the wine-making here is in the hands of an Englishman, Tim Manning – an idea which would have been preposterous to Ilaria Cavallini's grandparents. But Tim and Ilaria's brother, Antonio, are making a huge success of it, concentrating on the finest quality grapes from the small parcels of land, each with a different soil type and different grape varieties. "We practise small-batch fermentation here," says Tim. "Because we grow different varieties of grapes the harvest is a more long-winded and relaxed affair than elsewhere."

Tim is very serious about the organic aspect of their wine-making, and properly hostile to mono-culture. He has the full support of the family, with whom he works closely. The wine is Chianti Classico and Merlot. "We aim for quality not huge quantities," says Ilaria.

Il Borghetto is almost hidden; you could drive past and miss it, behind its tall hedges, private gates and lofty cypress trees. Slip inside and you feel you have stumbled upon a lost world. The main building is 15th century with pantile roofs sloping towards a central tower. The Cavallini family rescued it, along with the vineyards and olive groves, in 1982, with plans to live there and keep heads above water with the help of rooms for visitors. Much of the work, and most of the decorative ideas, came from Rosi, Ilaria's mother. Now, Ilaria and her husband Michele live on the estate and have taken up the reins. Father, Roberto, lives in Milan but comes back when he can, to his own house in the grounds.

They hold cookery classes in the superbly equipped modern kitchen, with its big mirrors for demonstrations. It is a beautiful old room, however, and still has a farmhouse feel to it: terracotta floors, marble sinks, high ceilings. Wine tasting courses are

offered, too, and dinner, as you would expect, is a treat that combines the best local foods and wines. Francesca Cianchi, the founding chef of New York's Mezzaluna restaurant, has held week-long courses here. Cookery tuition can be combined with art tours of Florence and Siena.

The whole place has been beautifully restored. The rooms have a timeless elegance, unshowy but rich and welcoming. The dining room opens airily onto a veranda, a fine place for breakfasts of brioche, local cheeses and homemade jams.

Bedrooms have tiled floors, stencil friezes, and beamed ceilings, and are understatedly luxurious with soft colours, antiques, fresh flowers and many individual touches – such as pretty wallpaper, or a

> "We practise small-batch fermentation and because we grow different varieties of grapes the harvest is a more relaxed affair than elsewhere"

sleigh bed, a writing desk or hand-painted wardrobe. They are all generous and comfortable, with good beds and their own bathrooms. There are French beds, antique family furniture, cotton fabrics in soft mellow colours. The top bedroom has magnificent views and there is a suite, too, with two bedrooms and two bathrooms; things have not been half-done. Bathrooms are simple, fresh and luxurious, with beams and uncluttered space.

There is a tidy garden with solar panels dotted about and little paths here and there. The kidney-shaped pool is hidden away. Beyond is a terraced water-garden and pond – and eye-stretching views. There is a herb garden, an orchard, and paths mown through the vineyards and olive groves.

Florence and Siena are close and staff will help you plan a trip, or borrow a bike and explore the surrounding countryside. But in the chapel of the Villa Caserotta near Calcinaia is a stunning 16th-century fresco by Ghirlandaio: wonderful art without the crowds. There is another gem right here: a 12th-century BC Etruscan tomb in the garden. It is one of the most ancient monuments in the Etruscan region and is said to be the final resting place of The Archer. To get a bird's-eye view of Chianti you can book a balloon trip in Tavarnelle.

Ilaria is very much in charge, and gets things done in spite of having two young daughters; Michele, her husband, is a guitarist and producer. They, along with Antonio and father Roberto, are a delightful family and their very typical Italian togetherness is a solid underpinning for their admirable Slow ambitions.

Antonio & Ilaria Cavallini

Azienda Agricola Il Borghetto,
via Collina 23, 50026 Montefiridolfi, San Casciano V.P
- 3 doubles, 5 suites. €130–€260.
- Dinner, 3 courses, €50. Wine €12–€80.
  Light lunch €15–€35.
- +39 0558 244442
- www.borghetto.org
- Train station: Florence

Fattoria Viticcio Agriturismo

TUSCANY

Nicoletta insisted on telling us the story behind the ubiquitous tiramisu dessert... it apparently has a noble history, having been created in Siena especially for Cosimo de Medici III at the end of the 17th century, to reflect all his 'qualities', such as 'importance' and 'strength'! It was christened the 'zuppa del Duca' and travelled to Venice where it was rapturously received by the courtesans, who ascribed aphrodisiacal properties to the humble dish and insisted on consuming it before their amorous encounters. Thus it gradually became known as 'tiramisu'... 'pick me up'.

As the name suggests, the Fattoria is a hard-working winery, not just a place dedicated to the gentle pampering of international guests. But that is why it is so rewarding to be there, for one feels part of the working 'thrub' of Tuscany rather than an uncomfortable interloper bent on idleness and introspection.

"He who is born under the vine has better luck than he who was born under the cabbage" goes the local saying. Put like that it is hard to disagree. Alessandro and Nicoletta do, genuinely, feel thrice blessed: by their vines, their countryside and their ability to welcome visitors. "Creating wines teaches you to be patient, to watch the wines mature in the barrels or bottles, to oversee every detail, to be aware of the effect they have on those who taste them." Visit the vaults and taste for yourselves. The wines have an international reputation – and deserve it. 200,000 bottles are produced annually.

The 35 hectares are planted with Sangiovese Grosso, Cabernet Sauvignon and Merlot grapes. There are more than 300 barrels of French and American white oak for the ageing of their super-Tuscans: the Prunaio, from the Grosso vines and Monile from Cabernet Sauvignon and Merlot.

Their vin santo is classically light and sweet. But the winery is known best, of course, for its Chianti Classico.

Agriturism can, like so many other phenomena, be little more than a label cynically attached to receiving people in the countryside. For these two delightful people it is much more, a way of bringing the countryside and its work into harmony with the outside world, of showing what agriculture means. They are proud that their wines reach across the globe to distant places, where people can learn, through tasting, about the reality of the production in Tuscany. They are, indeed, romantic about their wine-growing. Nicoletta, by the way, is a sommelier – and the oldest daughter, Beatrice, worked on a wine estate near Bordeaux and is studying viticulture.

Tiramisu
Serves 6–8

4 shots espresso
one box Pavesini cookies
4 eggs
2 tablespoons sugar
500g (1 lb) mascarpone
1 cup chocolate flakes
cocoa to dust

• Make the coffee and let it cool
• Lay the cookies in a serving dish and pour over the coffee
• Mix the eggs yolks and sugar
• Add in the mascarpone and then add in the beaten egg whites
• Spread half the cream mixture over the cookies
• Sprinkle dark chocolate flakes over the cream, then add the rest of the cream
• Dust with cocoa powder

Alessandro's father, Lucio, bought the farm in the 1960s, when others were leaving the land. The economy was in tatters, so it was a bold decision. The farm has prospered and the apartments are the icing on the cake. Delightful they are too: plain walls, beams, terracotta floor tiles, brick arches and a mixture of family furniture or pieces they have collected on their travels. They are big, light and airy, with superb kitchens with all you could possibly need – plus a superb hand-painted barrel top mounted on the wall. The daughters who play such a big role in the farm have given their names to the apartments: Beatrice, Arianna and Camilla. The simplicity of the rooms is just right for this farm. Some of the walls have wine-themed frescoes painted by young artists who gave their work in exchange for lodging.

You can reach this estate in just an hour by bus from Florence, and it is within walking distance of Greve in Chianti – the home of the CittaSlow movement. Greve's piazza is a gem with a loggia all round the square filled with artisan shops. People are given priority over cars, lighting the pavements priority over illuminating the sky, and local producers have seen off the big boys.

It is fitting that the Fattoria is part of the Slow scene of Greve. "'Viticcio' means 'tendril' in English," they explain. "It is symbolic of our slow and steady growth. Like the tendril we are carefully reaching new heights."

Alessandro Landini & Nicoletta Florio Deleuze

Fattoria Viticcio Agriturismo,
via San Cresci 12/a, 50022 Greve in Chianti
• 2 doubles, 1 twin. €100.
  5 apartments: 3 for 2–4, 2 for 4–6. €683–€970.
• Breakfast €5. Restaurants 15-minute walk.
• +39 055 854210
• www.fattoriaviticcio.com
• Train station: Florence

Locanda Casanuova

TUSCANY

Tuscany has always had a way of inspiring dreams; the Locanda Casanuova is a dream-maker. It is a place of contemplation, too, and always has been, for it began life as a monastery. Casanuova's bedrooms are almost monastically simple, but have splashes of colour and style to introduce a perfect measure of modernity. Another incarnation was as a farmhouse and the estate chapel is still there, for exhibitions and meditation.

The 23 hectares of vineyards and olives produce 7000 litres of wine and a lot of olive oil; there is an organic vegetable garden too.

Holland and Germany come together in Ursula and Thierry, she behind the smooth efficiency of the place, and in the kitchen with four helpers, and he, tanned and easy-going, in his supervision of the estate and the wine-making. They are fine hosts, smiley, humorous and generous – easy with themselves and their guests. He was a PE teacher; Ursula worked as a social worker in a female prison but was brought up on a farm. "That the land should be run on organic principles was the most important thing for us," says

Ursula, "and we were lucky that no chemicals had been used for a good number of years before we came. The land has now been managed organically for 50 years."

The atmosphere is wonderful for people who want to do their own thing unencumbered by hotelly expectations. They are right to call it a 'locanda' and not a hotel, for it has none of the mannerisms to be found in most hotels. It is an intensely personal place. It was 20 years ago that they came here and resolved to rescue it. They have done so much more: Ursula practises yoga in the early mornings – you are welcome to join her – and is a superb cook, the author of her own cookery book; meals are wonderfully convivial affairs in the refectory, off which is a library where you can pore over trekking maps at a big round table. Spontaneity is another feature; musicians, for example, might strike up at any moment on the terrace.

Ursula and Thierry rejoice in seeing their guests unfurl, the tension leaving them within days of arrival: "Those from towns and cities, particularly, arrive stressed. Often they will have planned an itinerary of sightseeing but relax into a different rhythm. In autumn, particularly, people love to get involved in the harvest. Spending time on the land and sharing a big spaghetti on the terrace at lunchtime can be really rewarding."

Just 500 yards from the house is a self-cleaning pond, set up as a swimming pool but rich in lily-pads and other vegetation. The light comes, dappled, through the branches of the lofty trees. The lovely garden has terraced steps, tables and delightful corners and nooks. Ursula is the goddess in the garden, as in the kitchen.

The area is densely forested with conifers; this eastern part of Tuscany is at a point where the cypress trees are giving way to another landscape. The views are far-reaching. You are close to Florence too, so you could, if you insist, burn yourselves up culturally with the greatest of ease.

There are two apartments, separate from the main house and down a bumpy track beside an ancient mulberry tree. They are rustically charming: attractive crocks, a collection of coffee pots and milk pans, candles and woodburner.

The mood of serene simplicity is at its most evident in the yoga room, a beautiful space with richly red silky curtains – a space that could lure even those most resistant to yoga.

The Casanuova is a natural candidate for Slow status, with its devotion to organics, its own vegetables, wine and olives, its lack of pretension and a commitment to doing things authentically. It also has that essential ingredient: great character.

Ursula & Thierry Besançon

Locanda Casanuova,
San Martino Altoreggi 52, 50063 Figline Valdarno
- 12 doubles, 2 suites, 4 singles. €90. Half-board €70 p.p. 2 apartments, €75–€100.
- Dinner €25–€30. Wine €8–€35.
- +39 0559 500027
- www.casanuova.info
- Train station: Figline Valdarno

Odina Agriturismo

TUSCANY

You are 650 metres above sea level here and will feel on top of the world. The Arno Valley stretches away in the distance, as do the Chianti hills, and air is as pure as can be. The house is a solid, stylish, pale-blue-shuttered place, run by Gloria who manages it all magnificently from her little office in the converted chapel.

If you arrive in a state of over-excitement, Valentina, the local herbalist who tends the magnificent herb garden, will perhaps recommend basil, which apparently helps with general restlessness – and sleeplessness, too. Having begun as a symbol of hatred in ancient Rome it became a symbol of love in Italy, with young maidens wearing a sprig in their hair to show that they were available for courtship.

Paolo, the proud owner, is a professional gardener and oversees the running of his herb farm 'con passione'. When he found Odina it was an abandoned medieval hamlet that he bought in its entirety. The self-catering apartments are all delightfully rustic and contemporary – the two styles cleverly combined. The overall effect is of softly muted colours, wood and sunlight. Each is different: some have kitchen surfaces of granite, others of local Pietra Serena. Bathroom walls are softly 'ragged' in varying shades. Each apartment has French windows to a patio with wooden garden furniture. In the de-consecrated chapel there is an old bread-making chest and a little shop selling Odina olive oil, beans, lavender and honey.

At the heart of Odina lies the organic herb garden, entered at each end through two rose-covered arches. Labels tell you about the medicinal and culinary uses of each plant and every week Valentina, a biologist, guides guests through the

garden to explain it all. Afterwards everyone prepares lunch together with freshly picked herbs and vegetables.

A dish from their little cookery leaflet is pasta with sardines and wild fennel, that delicious bulb that acts as an aid to digestion and is a breath sweetener. It was in the root of a fennel that Prometheus hid the spark of fire he had stolen from Mt Olympus. He was chained up for his crime and a vulture ate his liver. Those who know of the myth still consider it gauche to serve fennel with liver.

"Our British guests are intrigued by our herb garden," says Paolo. "Their interest is mostly in the

Spaghetti alla Crudaiola
Serves 1

5 cherry tomatoes
1 sprig each of fresh basil and parsley, chopped
1 teaspoon pine nuts, chopped roughly
1 tablespoon parmesan cheese
1 tablespoon extra virgin olive oil
half clove garlic, chopped
4–5 almonds, chopped
70g (3oz) spaghetti
chilli and salt to taste

• Chop the tomatoes, add basil and parsley then the pine nuts, cheese, oil, garlic and almonds
• Stir this mixture into just cooked spaghetti and stir
• Add chilli and salt to taste

Parsley: rich in vitamin C, a tonic and a diuretic
Basil: a relaxant and sedative
Chilli: a disinfectant, a digestive aid

much idling to be done. In the coolth of the early morning you may want to walk out into the hills and the surrounding woods, where Paolo has laid out paths for walkers. There are also longer trails for the hearty, and then there is the local organic food market in Montevarchi on a Saturday. Massage and reflexology can be arranged.

Paolo, Gloria and Valentina are passionate about their wider environment and they are planning to install energy systems using biomass, the sun and the wind. Naturally, the apartments have been restored using natural materials. He has done a magnificent restoration job. Says Gloria: "Paolo was very careful to use only old materials and local stone and wood in the conversion – it is the ultimate recycling project!"

culinary uses of the plants but the information that we lay out inspires them to consider their others uses, too."

Odina is one of those places which sap your will to move – there is so much to gaze upon, so

Signor Paolo Trenti

Odina Agriturismo,
loc. Odina, 52024 Loro Ciuffenna
• 4 apartments for 2–7, €550–€1,750.
  Farmhouse for 8–10, €2,050–€3,900. Prices per week.
• Restaurants 5km.
• +39 0559 69304
• www.odina.it
• Train station: Montevarchi

Agriturismo Rendola Riding

TUSCANY

Whether Jenny loves her horses, the Tuscan countryside or her guests most is hard to guess. She is a fascinating woman who embraced all things Italian when she moved here from England in the late 1960s. A dynamo, with a joie de vivre that seems to flourish in Italy, she sweeps everyone up into her enthusiasms.

Rendola is on the slopes of the Chianti hills, with 12 acres for 12 guests, 18 horses, paddocks and olive groves. Jenny pioneered equestrian tourism in Italy and thousands have come to ride with her – some having informal lessons in the ring surrounded by olive trees, some pottering gently along woodland tracks, some embarking on four- or five-day treks in the Chianti hills. For walkers there are many way-marked trails.

"People come back time and time again; we seem to have created something that appeals to a certain type of person. Rendola is not for those looking for elegance. Hens and ducks, never known for their respect for anyone's dignity, peck around the houses; our family dog, lies on the doorstep and jackets hang on the backs of chairs. It is first and foremost a riding centre and family home."

That is Jenny speaking – typically wanting to make sure that you understand the set-up and feel at ease. There is an absence of pomposity; you can just do your thing – whether in the garden, under a tree, or out on horseback.

"Guests quickly become friends," says Jenny, "and all who come – alone or with others – feel cherished. At meal times we sit together at a long table and there is plenty of merriment as well as good food." This is nourishing to hear – for Slow living needs a strong dose of conviviality. Imagine the scene at lunchtime: the outside world dozing in the sun, faint voices drifting up from the

vineyards, Tuscany working its magic upon another generation.

Jenny's team has been with her forever. There is Pietro – he with the red hat – who was a farmer between the 30s and 60s, before joining Jenny in 1970. He cooks simply, with home-reared turkeys and ducks and eggs, vegetables and oils and his son Sergio makes the puddings and can turn his hand to shoeing horses, building a wall, gardening and even installing a bathroom. Sergio's son, Marco, is a keen apprentice. Astonishing, in this age of fleeting phenomena, to have three generations working together.

"Pietro wrote his autobiography, *Pietro's Book* which was published in English in 2003. It's his answer to *Under a Tuscan Sun*," says Jenny. The book reveals the hardships and the joys of working on the land; Pietro's local knowledge is unmatched and it is a fortunate guest who can

> "At the end of each full and purposeful day a cow bell is rung and guests, family and stable workers gather to dine together"

speak Italian and engage him in conversation. There is a ride that takes guests along a section of an old Roman road on the way to Mercatale. Pietro remembers when it was paved over; the paving was destroyed by the passage of the Allied tanks in 1944. After the war local farmers took the seemingly humdrum stones home to use, not realising that among them were stones from the ancient Roman road.

The oak-beamed house is in the triangle formed by Florence, Arezzo and Siena, and is 1,000 feet above sea level. Jenny is keen, given how well-loved that area is already, to introduce people to 'Toscana Minore' – the landscape, history and art of her immediate surroundings.

Places such as the rose garden of Gropina Cavriglia, the largest in Europe, and a Romanesque church with a 9th-century pulpit. "We like to take people to places which they would have difficulty in finding on their own, which do not attract hordes of people and which are all the more fascinating and enjoyable for that."

To complete the happy band is Nicholas, Jenny's son, who edits an ecology magazine, *Terra Nuova*. He helps Jenny with her computer and occasionally entertains guests with his piano playing in the evenings. His touch is as light as Jenny's and guests hugely enjoy his company.

At the end of each full and purposeful day a cow bell is rung and guests, family and stable workers gather to dine together. If they are lucky, Pietro will be in the mood to round off the evening with a tale or two.

Jenny Bawtree

Agriturismo Rendola Riding,
Rendola 66, Montevarchi, 52025 Arezzo
- 3 twins/doubles, 2 family rooms, €90. 1 single, €50.
  Half-board €65 p.p. Full-board €85 p.p.
- Lunch or dinner €15–€20, with wine.
- +39 055 9707045
- www.rendolariding.it
- Train station: Montevarchi

Relais San Pietro in Polvano

TUSCANY

Just a short hop from Florence, by train and then a quick taxi ride, here is a Tuscan paradise easily reached by the Slow traveller. Yet it is wonderfully secluded, high up and blessed with everything that makes rural Tuscany so idyllic. Its elegance is bathed in dreamy views and it is inspired by the immensely likeable Luigi Protti. He is a real gentleman, and takes enormous, and understandable, pride in his creation of somewhere that is so special.

Luigi had been in Milan for 50 years when he decided to seek a country life for his family. Ever since then, he and Antonetta have carefully whittled their home to its present perfect form. Bedrooms have gorgeous old rafters, generous wrought-iron beds, elegantly painted wardrobes, rugs on tiled floors, handsome shutters. For cool autumn nights there are cream sofas and a log fire. The pool –

although not the Slowest of accoutrements – is worth mentioning for it must have one of the best views in Tuscany: keep your head above water and you are rewarded with the blue-tinted panorama for which Tuscany is famous. In summer you dine at tables dressed in white on a terrace overlooking the gardens and views of the olive-grove'd valley beyond. There is a restaurant, too, serving local food and their own olive oil; bread comes fresh from the bread oven, as do grissini dotted with poppy seeds.

Behind the scenes the cogs turn on oiled wheels. "Even with helpful staff and the support of the family it is not easy to run a small hotel," says Luigi. "We always ask guests what they particularly enjoy about their stay and our greatest pleasure is to receive notes of thanks from them. Our intention has been to offer a place of stillness and silence. There are paths and lanes

for walking and cycling and we are surrounded by small historical towns and villages.

"The family character of San Pietro is especially appreciated, as is the cooking and the tranquility. My wife and I run our small hotel equally with our son Franco and daughter-in-law Franca and we are all in agreement that we should keep the scale of things small – then we can manage everything ourselves. The same applies to our land: we have 500 olive trees that produce enough olive oil for us, our friends and guests."

It is a tenet of Slow that small is beautiful. Ernst Friedrich Schumacher – the true godfather of Slow? – proselytised that businesses and communities keep things local and on a human scale. Operating on a large scale, things can become unwieldy and large mistakes can be made... So it is a wise decision of the Prottis, and of many Italians in this book, to keep things in the family.

Spaghetti with Wild Fennel Sauce

320g (12.5 oz) spaghetti
150g (6oz) red onion, finely chopped
30g (1oz) fennel tops, chopped and blanched
30g (1oz) pine nuts
30g (1oz) raisins
chilli flakes, to taste
4 anchovies, chopped
white wine
salt, pepper and olive oil to taste

• Gently fry the onion, then add the fennel and fry for a few more minutes until soft
• Drown it all in the wine and add the pine nuts, raisins, chilli and anchovies. Cook for 10 minutes, stirring, until the wine evaporates
• Meanwhile boil the spaghetti and drain
• Take the spaghetti to the sauce and stir. Do not add parmesan!

Tuscany is alive with festivals and sagres – there is almost one for every month, so productive are the land and the farmers. There are sagres for wild boar, mushrooms, polenta, chestnuts, even steak! Open-air concerts at Cortona, Piero della Francesca's art in Arezzo and Sansepolcro and the monthly antiques fair in Arezzo could threaten to overfill your itinerary.

Castiglion, sitting smugly between the treasures of Siena, Florence and Perugia, overlooks the Val di Chio and the beginnings of the Appenines. It is an archaeologically significant town: the remains of what is thought to be a 4th-century BC Etruscan city wall were discovered under the Piazzale del Cassero. Castiglion is known locally for its annual Palio dei Rioni, held in the main piazza on the third Sunday of June. Horses representing different areas of the city race around the main square, as in Siena, but this Palio is considered less treacherous.

"We feel lucky to have landed in Castiglion Fiorentino. It is a friendly place and we find the people to be spontaneous, polite and open."

And that is exactly as guests have described this family, too. Those attributes and their tangible contentment create a quietly winning combination.

Signor Luigi Protti

Relais San Pietro in Polvano
loc. Polvano 3, 52043 Castiglion Fiorentino
- 10: 4 doubles, €130-€200, 1 single, €100-€120, 5 suites €200-€300.
- Dinner €20-€35. Wine from €14.
- +39 0575 650100
- www.polvano.com
- Train station: Castiglion Fiorentino, 8km

La Locanda

TUSCANY

Most guests arrive in a state of shock, admit Guido and Martina. The postal address suggests the Tuscan tourist trail, but the reality is glorious isolation. The Bevilacquas' skills as hosts soothe the most ruffled feathers, and the astonishing panorama of Chianti and the medieval village of Volpaia does the rest.

"We give guests an 'unplugged' experience without letting them feel abandoned," says Martina. "We look after them, make them drinks, cook for them, help them make plans. We know when to leave people alone and when to join in. The joy is that everyone is different, so our experience is always different. We expect to adjust to their needs, not the other way around."

Guido is an ex-banker and Martina worked in the Stock Exchange. They found the old farm 12 years ago after it had been abandoned for 40 years. "It was a classic story: farmhouse left to rot, trees growing inside, land overgrown," says Martina. "The fortunes of Tuscany were at an all-time low after the Second World War. People were deterred from farming here because of all the ups and downs of the landscape and the stony soil. There wasn't the equipment to maintain the slopes, the Chianti grape had no status in the world wine market and people left the area in droves looking for work."

Eventually the European economies picked up, many properties were re-organised into bigger farms and modern machinery made farming a good prospect once again.

"Smart people in the 70s saw an opportunity to own a part of this amazing landscape and began buying property and land, Agritourism started in the 80s, the area's reputation grew, and things turned around dramatically."

One would imagine, with the amalgamation of farmhouses into larger packages fit for selling,

that chaos would ensue over land ownership. But a Mediterranean generosity apparently reigns. Says Martina: "When you look at the hillsides you can see where one farmer's land ends and another's begins by looking at the way the crops are planted. But woods and forests are different. Here we are in the middle of a wood, there is no boundary but it really doesn't matter if it is my wood or my neighbour's. Our attitude is 'let's all enjoy it together!'"

There is a growing sense of responsibility towards the environment in Italy, some of it driven, of course, by economics. Many Italians, hit by expensive heating bills, are adjusting the

> "I prepare only one thing each night, just as you would at home. Sometimes we eat beautifully but simply, sometimes dinner is elaborate"

way they run their properties. "When we came here we were told that we couldn't install solar panels because they were ugly. Now we are encouraged by government grants to use them for pools and heating."

The couple are supporters of the Slow Food Movement and revel in the respect given to food, particularly here in central Italy. Says Guido: "We are surrounded by 300 hectares of some of the best organic vineyards, olive groves and honey. We take a lot of care choosing our suppliers and, thank God, here it is still possible to find small artisan producers." A particular favourite of theirs is the protected Cinta Sinese breed of pig. "It is the ultimate Slow food: the pigs are expensive to feed and take longer to grow, so they are not an economic choice of breed for the farmer," says Martina, "but the result is spectacular."

They can look after as many as 14 guests and there are no rules and no budgets to follow. Martina, who does most of the cooking, prepares what is seasonal and good. "I don't watch my shopping bill. I prepare only one thing each night, just as you would at home. Sometimes we eat beautifully but simply, sometimes dinner is elaborate. I don't stress about making profit from my cooking. I imagined when we moved here that we would find a local lady from the village to cook for us. She never materialised and now I do it all and I love it. I like to stay in the kitchen and be the background girl. Guido, who is Neapolitan, with a beautiful southern warmth, is very good at front of house."

They are a dynamic pair, full of vigour and life and have created a memorable place to stay. The beautiful pool vies for attention with the heart-stopping view, there are a library/bar, fine antiques, lovely art, whitewashed rafters soaring over pretty beds and terraces upon which Guido alights with glasses of wine, maybe a grappa, or a restorative coffee.

They have discovered their own 'tempo giusto' – the pace of life that suits them. They are vigilant guardians of the landscape and of local traditions. They richly deserve all the good company that is lured to La Locanda.

Guido & Martina Bevilacqua

La Locanda,
loc. Montanino di Volpaia, 53017 Radda in Chianti
- 3 doubles, 3 twins, 1 suite. €200–€300.
  Singles €180–€250.
- Dinner €35 (Mon, Wed & Fri only). Restaurants 4km.
- +39 0577 738832
- www.lalocanda.it
- Train station: Florence, 1hr

Fattoria Tregole

TUSCANY

What a spot! The mellow stone buildings are ringed by vines and woodland, with a high vantage point and long views over the Tuscan hills. Bolzano-born Edith and her architect husband Catello bought the rugged old farmhouse in the 1990s and transformed it into an idyllic place to stay.

As a professional art restorer, Edith had a keen interest in keeping the best of what is clearly a very ancient building. Its age was confirmed by the records of a local monastery, which showed that monks bought grain from Fattoria Tregole as long ago as 1003. The brick cellar, which now stores the Fattoria's precious stock of Chianti Classico, is 1,000 years old, as is a blunt tower now encased within newer parts of the house. The most unusual architectural feature is a 16th-century hexagonal chapel; ask Edith for the key as it's well worth having a look at the austere white-washed interior and the prettily peeling sky-blue paint of the dome. Throughout Fattoria Tregole though, sensitive use of stone, tile and wooden beams ensures that it's almost impossible to tell

the old parts of the building from the new extension.

Edith's approach within the building was admirably 'slow', and the results are both harmonious and elegant. Using traditional powdered paint, she mixed the colours herself, with rich terracotta, pale peach, deep olive green and soft sage hues reflecting the colours of the Tuscan landscape. Overlaying these sweeps of colour are stencilled oak leaves and trefoils, outlined with hand-painted swirls. And when you sink into a sofa you will be buoyed up by one of Edith's meticulously embroidered linen cushions, picked out in subtle, earthy tones.

Edith relishes her role as hostess and mixing her guests together, moves effortlessly between Italian, English and German. "I genuinely love people and I so enjoy having guests here, cooking and caring for them."

The main forum for conviviality at Fattoria Tregole is the twice-weekly dinner, eaten outside by candlelight on the terrace in summer. Edith says, "my guests come here to relax – and to eat! They can diet when they go home."

The long table groans with homemade food. You're likely

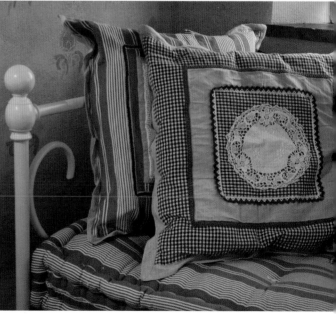

to be served a starter such as mushroom tart with crunchy bruschetta; a hearty pasta dish, perhaps Edith's classic pasta with zucchini and bright dashes of yellow zucchini flowers; a meat course which might be wild boar hunted in the nearby woods; and a fruit tart. All the food is, needless to say, local, seasonal and cooked with their own olive oil, and much of it comes from Edith's neat vegetable garden, which is edged around with bold, bright dahlias and climbing roses.

Food is a real feature of a visit here, and one of Edith's many passions. Join in with a cooking class that starts at 5pm and ends with the sharing of an evening meal. "Good food and wine bring people together," Edith says. Choosing wines to accompany the excellent food is Catello's considerable contribution to proceedings. His Chianti Classico made from Sangiovese grapes is

> ## "Catello's Chianti Classico is reckoned to be one of the thirty best wines in Tuscany"

reckoned by the Camera di Commercio in Siena to be one of the 30 best wines in Tuscany. There's a lot of competition from excellent winemakers, so you can be sure this is the real deal. You might also want to sample their own vin santo and grappa, a fire-water spirit.

Edith marks out the year with jam-making: marmalade is made in winter, next comes quince jam, and then strawberry, apricot and fig. All these await you on the breakfast table, as will homemade yoghurt and a freshly baked cake.

You're in beautiful Chianti country and the hill towns and vineyards reward exploration; smart Castellina in Chianti is just 4km away and has substantial Etruscan remains; tiny Radda in Chianti has an absorbing early medieval core.

The nearby village of Panzano looks out at the Golden Valley (Conca d'Oro) and has the fine Romanesque church of Pieve di San Leolino. Panzano has been called paese dei golosi (village of gourmands) and at its spiritual heart is the 250-year-old butchery, Antica Macelleria Cecchini. As you wait in line you can taste their specialities, maybe sip wine and listen to classical music. It's an institution and owner Dario a legend.

Siena, of course, holds some of the greatest works of the Renaissance: Martini's glittering Maestà; Ambrogio Lorenzetti's Allegories of Good and Bad Government which depict the 14th-century city; Pinturicchio's dramatic fresco in the Piccolomini Library in the duomo. Having explored the medieval masterpiece that is Siena, it is delightful to return to Fattoria Tregole. Thanks to the creative flair of Edith and Catello it is, in a quiet way, a work of art in itself.

Edith Kirchlechner

Fattoria Tregole,
loc. Tregole 86, 53011 Castellina in Chianti
* 4 doubles, €130. 1 suite for 2, €180.
  2 apartments: 1 for 4, 1 for 5. €200–€320.
* Dinner €35, by arrangement. Wine from €10.
* +39 0577 740991
* www.fattoria-tregole.com
* Train station: Siena

Frances' Lodge

TUSCANY

"No pictures can match the beauty," says Frances Mugnai about her home. The sheer loveliness of their farm, the space, the colours, the cool breezes, make being here something special. It is a wonder that it is so peaceful yet so close to Siena; apparently, when the Palio is about to start you can hear the mounting excitement of the crowd that is packed into the medieval walled city just across the way.

It is a ten-minute bus ride to Siena and its campo, the main tower of which, the Torre del Mangia, stands proud of the city's roofscape. The hill-top lemon-coloured house and farmhouse, which belonged to the nearby 18th-century manor, was converted by Frances' family as a summer retreat. The lofty, light-filled limonaia (lemon house) is filled with beautiful things: vibrant art, deep sofas, and oriental touches.

It is a place of enormous beauty yet has its feet firmly planted in the traditions of Tuscany. Indeed, Franco is from a long line of Tuscans. In its eight acres of land – eight acres so close to Siena! – there are olive, lemon and quince groves and numerous fruit trees. From the fruits, Frances makes jams of every flavour. As for so many Italian cooks, recreating peasant dishes is a matter of pride for her – Pappa al Pomodoro for instance. "Even the poorest families had their own tomatoes, olive oil and leftover bread. It is a labour of love, it needs attention, but how beautiful it is."

Frances' new passion is saffron. There is one harvest in October each year and, when the crocus bulbs are ready, friends, family and the community roll up their sleeves to help. "We don't produce enough to employ a team but, because we need to work quickly, even with a smallish harvest we need help." Each bulb produces three flowers, with three strands of saffron to each

flower. During the ten-day blossoming the flowers have to be picked early each morning. A swift harvest is essential.

"We rise early and race the birds to the flowers," says Frances. "They are taken in a basket to the kitchen and we remove the saffron stems straight away. Then we dry them, near the fire in the winter and in a very low oven in the summer." Frances began her experiment with saffron in 2004 and last year she had a whopping crop of 200g. By 2008 she was the chosen supplier to the best restaurant in Siena.

Risotto alla Milanese is Frances' favourite dish for the prized ingredient – "saffron is the protaganist, the main flavour of the dish". She infuses the saffron in boiled water for 20 minutes to release the flavour, removes the stems (keeping

"Their own olive oil is decanted into little bottles for guests to take home"

them for decoration) and then cooks her rice in the flavoured water. Guests, in raptures – we are told – over the flavours, go home with little packets of the flower to which Frances has pinned the recipe.

Their own olive oil is decanted into little bottles for guests to take home, too – as is her potent limoncello made with her own organic lemons. Some of her lemon trees are 150 years old and planted in handmade terracotta pots. They are used decoratively, in the 16th-century tradition of Italian garden design.

Three lemon harvests a year and a late-October ripening of olives provoke another flurry of activity as the groves come alive with friends coming and going. Everyone gathers for lunch and dinner on the terraces for restorative plates of pasta. It's a sociable and productive time of year; the guests have gone and the crops dictate the rhythms of life.

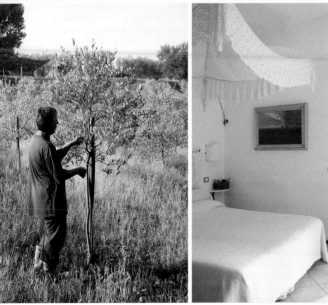

Frances dug a well to help irrigate the land – "I don't like to use water from the tap for the gardens". Solar panels heat water for big chunks of the year and she has 'forever' had low-energy lighting, timer switches and sensors to cut down on her use of power.

The pool reflects the views of the city skyline; the loggia opens onto fields of wheat and the smell of rose, wisteria and lemon blossom drift around your breakfast table. The garden designer, A. Fantastici, introduced a touch of fantasy with the elegant birdcage temple in the early 19th century.

Franco, like every self-respecting Sienese, is a fanatical supporter of the Palio where Contradas (districts) battle for supremacy in the twice-yearly horse race around the Piazza del Campo; people take up their positions days before the 73-second race. "His Contrada is the 'Torre' and its flags hang in the house. The other Contradas have historically fought about boundaries," explains Frances, "but the Torre's interests are not in this; its biggest adversary is 'Oca' and they battle for prestige."

The winning Contrada pays dearly for the victory as it has to pay its jockey, handsomely, and pay bribes to other riders for their 'help'. If you can't win, you then hope that your biggest enemy doesn't win.

Best of all, they will come second – to come second in the Palio, many say, is to come last.

Franca Mugnai

Frances' Lodge, strada di Valdipugna 2, 53100 Siena
* 3 doubles, €180–€220.
  2 suites (1 for 2, 1 for 4), €240.
  Min. stay 2 nights; 3 nights during the Palio.
* Restaurants 1km–2km.
* +39 0577 281061
* www.franceslodge.it
* Train station: Siena

Podere Salicotto

TUSCANY

Relaxation requires effort and even in the bucolic setting of Salicotto, it isn't always easily attained.

"Guests arrive after hectic journeys and discover how different our rhythms are. The first thing that strikes them is the silence. It can be overwhelming for some and we understand that it takes time to adjust."

Silvia and Paolo moved here from Milan in 2004 – they had demanding careers, busy social lives, and threw in, for good measure, the odd challenging cross-Atlantic sailing trip on their Hallberg Rassy boat. A three-year search for a new home in the country ended with a drive up to this 1820 farmhouse in Le Crete Senesi. It is 3km from Buonconvento, a thriving little town, but set apart from – well, everything.

"The most surprising thing to us was the all-enveloping silence. But I have learned to love the peace and now I crave it; silence makes space for new thoughts and that is a gift."

They began the hard work of renovating the two dwellings using local labour and materials and created six bedrooms and one apartment for guests. The beamed and

terracotta-tiled bedrooms are airy and pleasing, full of soft, Tuscan colours and furnished with simplicity: antiques, monogrammed sheets, great showers. Wherever you turn the Tuscan landscape is laid out for you to admire for there are 360-degree views on top of the hill here.

From the poolside you can see Montalcino to the south and Siena to the north; there are plenty of garden seats all around for you to sit and absorb the colours, the smells and the wildlife. Emerging from the wood you may see a deer with her fawns; in the early morning watch the mists lifting as the temperature rises; in the evening the moonrise – Paolo says it is magical.

The organic farmland is spread over 46 acres and they produce organic grass for animal feed, walnuts, maple trees and, elsewhere, they grow olives and vines, too. There is a modern cellar that looks more like a smart shop where bottled oils and wines are kept. Everything feels polished and well-run yet Silvia and Paolo's feet are firmly rooted in the traditions of their community.

They join in with the local festivals – in Buonconvento

Il Rigo
TUSCANY

The best cooks have the most fun with food. Not for them precision measuring and anxious minutes looking through the glass door of the oven. They understand what works with what, how things react and work or don't work; they experiment and go on building their skills.

Lorenza, one senses, has always been this way with food. She runs a cookery school in San Quirico d'Orcia, has taught in the States and is master of the menus at Il Rigo. "I love playing with pasta," she says. "I can change the proportions, the colours, the stuffings and the flour, and create hundreds of different flavours. I like making puddings, too, and cakes, so flour is my number one ingredient."

Lorenza celebrates amateurism in the kitchen; she would hate to think of everyone being trained.

"Over-education is the enemy of tradition," she says and the seasons are her guide to ingredients. "I would never use pecorino at the end of the summer, for instance. It's not fresh enough and the milk has a different flavour from the milk of spring, during the lambing season. It is rewarding to find the perfect seasonal partner for food. Nature dishes up perfect combinations, like an early crop of figs to go so perfectly with that pecorino. I am careful to get regionality right, too. Although I am Ligurian and love pesto I would hesitate to serve basil pesto because it is not a Tuscan dish and my guests from Liguria would notice!"

In spring Lorenza takes her cookery students to see that pecorino being made in nearby Pienza; in October they visit saffron farms together. Wild boar and venison appear on the menu in winter. Year round their farm supplies them with vegetables – greens, courgettes, peppers, salad leaves and tomatoes.

The Orcia valley is a Unesco World Heritage site. The hills are of soft clay, the cornfields a

swaying sea of golden ochre; the landscape displays the full palate of Tuscan colours. There are two farmhouses on the hill: Casabianca,

Cantucci with Almonds

600g (1lb 5oz) plain flour
pinch salt
8g (1 teaspoon) baking powder
500g (1lb 1oz) sugar
3 whole eggs
2 egg yolks
little glass vin santo
lemon or orange zest
300g (11oz) almonds in skin, lightly toasted
1 egg yolk to brush over biscotti

• Mix flour, salt, baking powder and sugar
• Using only the top of your finger, mix in eggs and yolks and vin santo
• Add zest and almonds – you may need a bit of flour on your hands
• Make snakes about 4cm wide, 2cm high
• Place on buttered and floured baking tray and brush surface with yolk
• Cook for 30 minutes at 180°C (350°F/Gas 4), cut into pieces, then cook for further 10 minutes. These keep well in an airtight tin. Good with coffee or vin santo.

dating from 1572, with nine rooms, and Poggio Bacoca, with six rooms. Each is rustic, woody, simple but with enough stylish touches to enchant us all. There are embroidered sheets, flowered bedspreads, gleaming white bathrooms. Everyone eats at Casabianca or drops by the *cantina* for wine tasting and exquisite seasonal snacks. There is a wood-fired oven in the courtyard.

Breakfast ciambellone (cakes) are home-made, as is the pasta. There are bruschetta and cold meats and cheeses for lunch, cantucci to go with a

glass of vin santo. You will eat like a king, led astray, not least, by the 60 wines in their cellar.

The couple were married 20 years ago – the cypress trees that line the drive were a wedding present – and their contentment is palpable. Their

"Nature dishes up perfect combinations, like an early crop of figs to go so perfectly with fresh pecorino"

delight at being guardians of Vittorio's old family home transfers itself to guests. "Life is busy but when I am in my car on my way to town to shop or to the cookery school, I look every day at the landscape as a newcomer. When the light is beautiful I am happy for my guests – happy that they can share the beauty."

Guests staying at Poggio Bacoca farmhouse walk up to Casabianca to use the pool, or to eat. Lorenza asked a friend who works with wood to carve a sign to entertain them on the way. By the side of the track you come across an extract of a passage from Dante's Divine Comedy: "What negligence, what standing still is this? Run to the mountain to strip off the slough that lets not God be manifest to you."

Signor Vittorio Cipolla & Lorenza Santo

Il Rigo,
Podere Casabianca, 53027 San Quirico d'Orcia
- 15 doubles, €100–€110.
  Half-board €144–€156 p.p.
- Lunch or dinner €22–€25, by arrangement.
- +39 0577 897291
- www.agriturismoilrigo.com
- Train station: Buonconvento, 15km

Podere le Mezzelune

TUSCANY

Just where the hills rise from the plains above the ports of Livorno and Piombino, you will find Podere le Mezzelune. This is the region of Maremma, and from here views reach as far as the islands of Elba, Gorgona and even Corsica.

The Maremma is fascinating, and curiously ignored by the many travellers who pass by on their way to the more celebrated parts of Tuscany. All Italians think regionally rather than nationally and are fiercely protective of their birthplace, but here in Tuscany, those that live in the Maremma feel that their tiny corner of western Tuscany is its own universe. Italy is a nation of mini-universes.

Over 2,000 olive trees and 15 hectares of land surround le Mezzelune, and add to the magical seclusion of the place, gazing from the hills down to the coast. Luisa arrived in 1985 and has pulled off a triumphant restoration. She is a gifted designer – fabrics are her thing – and a calm

emanates from the podere's interior: white muslin billows in the breeze, a delicate light filters into the bedrooms and well-chosen furniture decorates, rather than overpowers, the spaces. Upstairs are four bedrooms, two looking out to sea, private and secluded with their own fine views from their terraces. They have linen curtains, wooden floors, furniture made to Luisa's design, good fabrics, candles, fresh fruit and, maybe, vintage wooden pegs hung with an antique shawl. Colours are calming neutrals – a gentle mix of beige, taupe, cream. Bathrooms, too, are perfect. For longer stays there are two little private cottages in the garden with all the gadgets and equipment you could possibly need along with open fires, beams, sofas piled with cushions and lovely beds. Luisa created it all with her late husband Sergio. When he died Luisa decided to share the running of it with her friend, Renata.

An important part of their plan is for their farmland to be granted official organic status. Says Renata: "We produce our own IGP-labelled olive oil but for our farm to achieve organic status we have to convince our neighbours to become organic, too. We have received recognition from the Slow Food Movement, which makes us very proud for they set the standard for all to follow. We use traditional methods of crushing the olives between large stones. The result," says Luisa, "is a sweet oil with a light bitter aftertaste. The oils are shiny with golden yellow colours and green reflective lights." The bottles are artfully displayed in the *bottega*, alongside bottles of preserved aubergines, courgettes and tomatoes from the kitchen garden.

The orchard produces lemons, peaches, cherries and strawberries – all to be found on the breakfast table, with charcuterie, cheeses and home-made cakes. Napkins are tied with twine and a sprig of lavender; this attention to detail is delightful.

The house has been heated, thus far, by a boiler fed with the estate's coppiced wood. "One of our ambitions is to protect our natural environment," says Renata. "A respect for nature should be at the core of all we do. It is worrying to see rapidly developing countries without a respect for the foundation of its culture. Europe is so green and beautiful; it could be regarded as the garden of the world. We have been blessed with this landscape and now we know how best to protect it. We all have a duty to be part of that preservation."

Luisa Chiesa Alfieri

Podere le Mezzelune,
via Mezzelune 126, 57020 Bibbona
- 4 twins/doubles, €166–€176.
  2 cottages for 2, €166–€176.
- Restaurants 3km.
- +39 0586 670266
- www.lemezzelune.it
- Train station: Cecina

Pieve di Caminino

TUSCANY

As pilgrims found shelter and warmth here 1,000 years ago, so will you. Pieve di Caminino is a former romanesque church, its existence first recorded in the 11th century. It is built on Paleo-Christian ruins and it is said that three saints lived here: Feriolo, Egenziano, who met his end in Africa, and Luca who turned the abandoned monastery into an agnostic hermitage. At the site of Feriolo's death, it was said, a spring sprung forth and from then on even more pilgrims would come to stay at this 'miraculous' hamlet.

The estate has been in Piero's family since 1872 and from that time the land, buildings and community have been thoroughly restored. Antonio Giuseppe Marrucchi created a hamlet in which farm-workers would work and live and, following in the footsteps of the monks who produced oil here, he planted new olive trees, some of which are still here. By the 1960s Caminino was almost

deserted again as workers left for the cities – a theme common in this book. The farm limped on until the Marrucchi Locatelli arm of the family took over in 1983.

The setting is dramatic – the landscape forms a natural amphitheatre that on one side slopes down to the west coast of Italy; the Castiglione della Pescaia beach is a beautiful surprise for visitors, as are the sea views from here on a clear day. There are 500 hectares of farmland with olive groves, vineyards and a cork tree forest.

You drive through the big rusty gates and down the tree-lined drive to be greeted by Emiliano in what must be the most beautiful 'reception' in the book. These are their private quarters, lined with paintings by famous Locatelli artists. Among soaring columns. stone arches and vaulted ceilings you may well be invited to taste the estate's extra virgin olive oil. They have been

pressing their oil since 1872 and they serve it with toasted bread touched by garlic and salt. With a glass of red wine in hand, you can wander, feeling a touch diminished by the lofty surroundings.

Piero and son Emiliano are both heritage architects, working in Florence and at studios here. The Pieve has been the subject of dissertations by seven PhD students and the son and father have personally assisted each in their studies.

"I love our farmland but I regard it as a frame for the house. I know every inch of this place. Historical societies have used it as an archaeological, not an architectural, study. I have measured and know every stone and every tile."

As much thought has gone into the preservation of the eco-system as of the Pieve and the apartments. Deer, wild boar, the many birds,

> "Pieve is not a business, it is part of our family. I want to look after it myself"

butterflies, snakes and lizards are evidence of sympathetic land management, and Emiliano has created hides in the woods where you can observe the wildlife for yourself. Wildlife aside, the Maremma, in Tuscany's south western corner, is a fascinating region. It is 70% forest and has the lowest population density of all Tuscan areas. "There has been virtually no bad land usage," says Emiliano, "no big roads were built here and no airports. There aren't even any traffic lights!" Indeed, it is hard not to conclude that the motor car has led the historical assault on Slow.

"It is Slow – too Slow for some. It can take weeks to find a plumber or a workman. I explain to my guests that Slow Food restaurants can be slow through and through so that they go prepared for a wait and they are accepting! When my father came here in the 70s to hunt he would have to leave his car a good way away and ride a horse the last bit

of the journey. There was no electricity until the 80s and if he wanted to watch a soccer match he had to connect the television to the car battery.

"Thanks to technology I can live and work here. Very few houses come up for sale in the Maremma – those who live here realise how lucky they are. The clean air alone is a good enough reason to choose the area; the space, the peace and the coast make it exceptional.

"There are no televisions and no internet connection in the apartments," says Emiliano, "we want to encourage people to 'staccare la spina' – relax their spine – and spend their time quietly. To continue the Slow theme, we only suggest visits to outposts that are little-known, places where guests can get to know genuinely local restaurants that are family-run and where there may be only one dish on offer, cooked for you by the owners."

Emiliano's connection with the area is strong; his wife, Chiara, is the daughter of the famous Moris winemaking family and he has always hunted with her father. Now their daughter, Benedetta, will see her parents care for Pieve just as Emiliano watched Piero and Daniela.

"Pieve is not a business, it is part of our family. I want to look after it myself, which is why I am here 99% of the time to greet guests personally," says Emiliano. "I have had the loveliest people working with me but it is best when I do it. I light fires in the apartments, I lay out chocolates, I work hard to make sure that everyone is happy."

Famiglia Marrucchi Locatelli

Pieve di Caminino,
Strada Provinciale 89, Peruzzo, 58036 Roccatederighi

* 5 suites for 2–3, €120–€160. 2 apartments for 4.
* Breakfast €10. Restaurant 6km.
* +39 0564 569736
* www.caminino.com
* Train station: Grosseto

Il Pardini's Hermitage

TUSCANY

If you are alone, the family invites you to eat with them. When you relax in the garden, Federigo may appear, unprompted, with a glass of chilled wine. When you arrive, music is chosen for you and when you leave the family comes to the boat to wave you off.

Il Pardini's Hermitage is an institution, a heart-winner, an exceptional place in so many ways. The spirit of inclusion, openness and gentleness is second to none and the seclusion and necessary self-sufficiency create a thriving community. Deftly, guests are helped to feel part of it all.

This is much more than a place to stay. You can learn to paint, throw pots, do yoga or cookery courses, play music, meditate. Or just find your own quiet space to read and enjoy the garden. The occasional yoga chant may catch the breeze and drift your way, further adding to the meditative air.

Tantalisingly close to the Tuscan coastline, Isola del Giglio is a 60-minute boat ride from the mainland but a world away. Once you arrive, a small boat then picks you up from Giglio Porto for the 20-minute journey round to the rocky outcrop beneath Pardini. If the weather isn't good, the brochure says, "the hotel can be reached on foot via a one and a half hour walk on uneasy paths". Now you get a sense of the seclusion; a journey here could feel like a pilgrimage, and many before you have done it on a donkey.

Barbara's great grandfather came from Giglio and her family talked wistfully of their blissful life there. Federigo, whose father started Pardini, met Barbara when she was working in a bank in Geneva. His tales of island life mirrored the fond memories she had gleaned from her grandfather and it took little persuasion to get her out to the island to see the house where Federigo's father

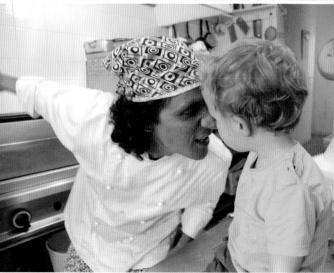

PARDINI,S
HERMITAGE

built a little house for family holidays. That was in 1962 and by 1966 the couple had moved to Giglio to help welcome guests in the, by then, much-extended Hermitage. It is not a house of cossetting luxury or poly-starred facilities – there is a satisfying and very human assortment of family furniture, simple bedrooms, cool tiled floors – but you sense how it has grown organically and how much it is loved by the family.

"Every summer our daughter Veronica stays for three months with her young son Orlando; her cousin Antonio helps me to cook; Rosy, our friend, works in the office and helps us create a special atmosphere for the guests," says Barbara. "We respect that all our guests are different and need different things – we try to recognise what would

> "We respect that all our guests are different and need different things – we try to recognise what would make them more happy"

make them more happy. Giglio is more relaxed than the rest of Italy and we enjoy the fact that we have contact with guests. In big hotels sometimes nobody talks with each other."

Federigo's joie de vivre is evident at all times – especially when showing guests his garden that tumbles down the rockface towards the sea. He has terraces and vines, tomato plants and salad crops. Barbara copes with gluts of vegetables with aplomb: boxes of aubergines are sliced, baked and layered with cheese, tomatoes and courgettes for melanzana parmigiana; plentiful salads are a welcome light lunch for guests who gather on the terrace that seems to jut out over the sea. The small kitchen produces some spectacular meals, mostly made with home produce. "We have no menus but guests choose from a spread laid out in the dining room. We have lots of seafood and our own meats, too."

Federigo and Barbara together look after 11 donkeys, 35 goats and 20 pigs. They are all treated as pets although their presence comes from a practical need and desire for self-sufficiency. The Amiata donkeys are used when boats can't reach this side of the island, goat's milk is used by the cooks, and the pigs – an ancient Cinta Sinese breed – are slaughtered for prosciutto and Finnocchiona, a special type of Tuscan salami made with home-grown fennel.

Drinks are taken together before dinner, with friends family and guests gathering after the activities of their day. After dinner you can gather for a limoncello or port and, often, an impromptu music recital. Veronica says "The rhythm here is 'lento'. We encourage guests to stay for a week. It takes time to get into it, but once they do, guests come back time and time again."

Federigo & Barbara Pardini

Il Pardini's Hermitage,
loc. Cala degli Alberi, 58013 Isola del Giglio
- 10 doubles, 2 singles, 1 suite.
  Half-board €95–€155 p.p. Full-board €130–€180 p.p.
- Wine from €15.
- +39 0564 809034
- www.hermit.it
- Train station: Orbetello

Le Marche   Umbria   Lazio

[CENTRAL]

CENTRAL

Arcing across the Italian peninsular, this band of regions has the majestic Apennine Mountains at its core. Le Marche borders the Adriatic and stretches across a long narrow coastal plain with rolling countryside that is cut off by wild and inaccessible peaks. Lazio has a rich historic and architectural heritage and a long coastline of dunes, salt marshes and pine forests facing the Tyrrhenian Sea. Evergreen, landlocked, Umbria nestles between.

The lusty, mysterious Etruscans ruled central Italy before the rise of Rome but they ventured no further east than Umbria. The Romans then built roads across the Apennines to establish colonies in Le Marche. After the fall of Rome, Goths and Byzantines struggled for supremacy. The Longobardi followed, then the Papacy ruled, apart from a brief period when the French took over before Italy became a unified kingdom in 1860. Lazio was finally annexed in 1871.

Le Marche's Adriatic coast is known for its regimented sandy beaches. However, Monte Conero is edged by small bays and coves, backed by steep white tree-covered cliffs. Mezzavalle is only accessible on foot and Le Due Sorelle by boat. Portonovo has a busy but pretty beach and a landing place for fishing boats making it the perfect place to try the local *brodetto* (fish soup), mussels and other seafood dishes. After lunch visit the 11th-century Romanesque church that sits peacefully among evergreen oaks.

There are walking, trekking, hunting and fishing opportunities in the regional and national parks. You may glimpse the swoop of golden eagles, spot a wild boar or even catch sight of the timid lynx or brown bear; both have returned to the Sibillini Mountains. There are *sagres* (food festivals) dedicated to many foods, including the *lumaca* (snail) the *vincisgrassi* (local lasagne), the *tartuffo bianco* (white truffle).

"the lusty Etruscans ruled here before the rise of Rome"

Porchetta, the whole roast baby suckling pig, is a regional speciality. The local Verdicchio or Bianchello wines go well with seafood, Rosso Conero with meat.

Pesaro, the birthplace of Rossini, holds an international festival of his music every year in August. Macerata's renowned neo-classical Sferisterio, a columned semi-circular outdoor arena, holds 7,000 spectators for the opera season in July and August. Urbino, the Renaissance capital, stages a festival of ancient music in front of the Palazzo Ducale, one of Italy's finest.

The Piazza del Popolo, the elegant main square of the medieval city of Ascoli Piceno, is an animated place for an *aperitivo* and olive *ascolane* (stuffed and deep fried) while watching the locals. The town, like so many others, has wonderful gothic buildings, fascinating galleries and good shopping.

Umbria is at the heart of the Italian Peninsular. Its gentle landscape of fertile hills, forests, fortified hilltop towns and mountains has 30 bike trails though a mystic, spiritual and leafy land. The Marmore Falls are staggering and provide enough hydroelectricity to power the region's steel industry.

You can, if you are a rambler or aspiring saint, follow in the footsteps of Saint Francis, *il poverello d'Assisi.* Take the path he trod in 1207 from Assisi to Gubbio and walk though a living Renaissance fresco of soft colours and dramatic backdrops, stopping off to enjoy the sacred architecture and paintings.

Perugia is the home of the famous university for foreign students and hosts the Euro Chocolate Fair in October; the town has the lovely Palazzo Priori and Fontana Maggiore at its centre.

This land dotted with ancient castles has a deep farming culture; wheat, olives, sunflowers and grapes thrive. A black truffle fair is held in Norcia every February; lentils are grown around nearby Castelluccio, an ancient village in spectacular mountains.

The lively, walled 14th-century town of Montefalco, the 'balcony of Umbria', has panoramic views across the region and a wine festival in September to show off the locally made Sagrantino di Montefalco. Città della Pieve parades in August, in Renaissance costume inspired by Perugino's paintings; Todi hosts an arts festival and Foligno a jousting tournament.

Lazio is somewhat overshadowed by Rome yet holds many treasures; you can go 'archeo-trekking' around the ancient sites of the Etruscan cities of Vulci, Tarquinia, Veio and Cervetri and visit il Lago di Bolsena and Sutri with its magnificent amphitheatre.

Go to Rome in January and you will tussle with the locals at the winter sales. Culture and fun comes cut-price, too: entry to museums and galleries, concert hall tickets and river trips are all discounted.

Sunsets in Rome can be spectacular. Go to Piazza Campidglio to admire the Roman Emperor Marco Aurelio on horseback, climb the elegant double stairway and look down on the symmetry of the square laid out by Michelangelo. Then walk behind the palazzo and take in the whole of the Roman Forum that stretches out before you in the dying sun.

There are ways of escaping the bustle. Take off for the peace of Villa Adriana where you can lose yourself among the shady ruins. This is Hadrian's (of wall fame) vast architectural playground, his country residence in the foothills of the Tiburtino mountains. Nemi, an enchanting hill-top town overlooking a volcanic lake of the same name, is famous for its perfumed wild strawberries. In June it is decked in flowers during the Fragola Profumata festival.

Lindy Wildsmith

CENTRAL

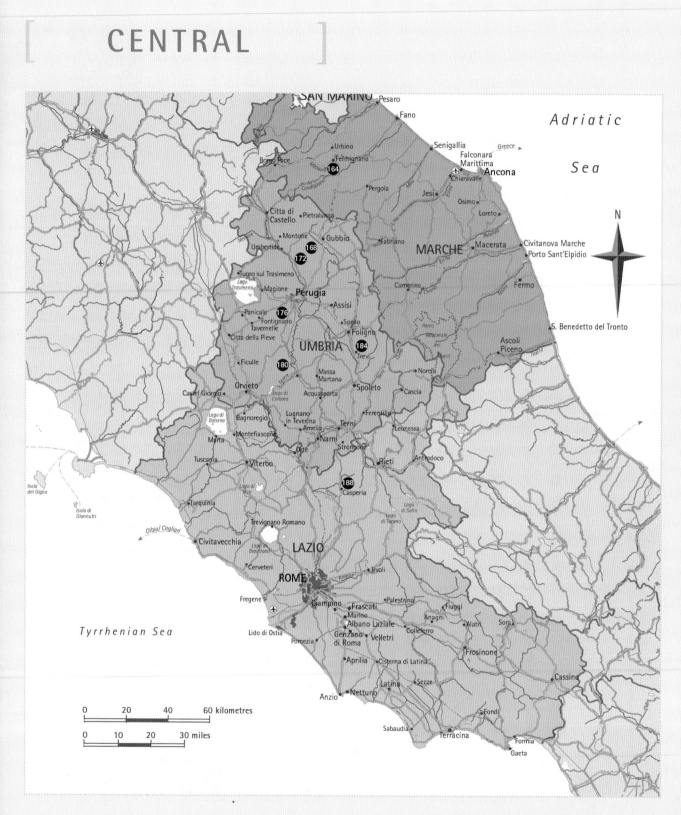

SAN MARINO

Adriatic

Sea

Pesaro

Fano

Greece →

Urbino
Senigallia

Borgo Pace
Fermignano
164

Falconara
Marittima

Ancona

Pergola
Chiaravalle

Jesi

Osimo
Citta di
Castello
Pietralunga

Loreto

Montone
Gubbio

Umbertide
168
Fabriano
MARCHE
Macerata
Civitanova Marche

172
Porto Sant'Elpidio

Tuoro sul Trasimeno
Camerino

Fermo
Lago
Trasimeno
Magione

Perugia
Assisi
Panicale
176

Fontignano
Spello
S. Benedetto del Tronto
Tavernelle
Foligno
Citta della Pieve
UMBRIA
184
Ascoli
Piceno
Ficulle
Trevi
180
Parco

Massa
Nazionale
Martana
Norcia
dei

Orvieto
Acquasparta
Spoleto
Monti
Castel Giorgio
Cascia

Lago di
Corbara
Lugnano
Ferentillo

Bagnoregio
in Teverina
Terni
Leonessa

Lago di
Amelia
Bolsena
Montefiascone
Narni

Marta
Orte
Stroncone
Antrodoco

Tuscania
Rieti

Viterbo

Lago di
Vico
188
Lago
di Salto
Tarquinia
Casperia

Isola
del Giglio

Lago
Isola di
di Turano
Giannutri

Trevignano Romano

Olbia/ Cagliari →

Civitavecchia
Lago di
Bracciano
LAZIO

Cerveteri
ROME
Tivoli

Fregene
Palestrina
Fiuggi
Ciampino
Frascati
Marino
Anagni
Alatri
Sora
Albano Laziale
Colleferro
Lido di Ostia
Genzano
Velletri
di Roma
Tyrrhenian Sea
Frosinone
Pomezia
Aprilia
Cisterna di Latina
Cassino
Latina
Sezze
Anzio
Nettuno
Fondi
Sabaudia
Terracina
Formia
Gaeta

N

0   20   40   60 kilometres

0   10   20   30 miles

Special places to stay

Le Marche

164   Locanda della Valle Nuova

Umbria

168   Locanda del Gallo

172   Casa San Gabriel

176   Villa Aureli

180   La Palazzetta del Vescovo

184   I Mandorli Agriturismo

Lazio

188   La Torretta

Locanda della Valle Nuova

LE MARCHE

The Savinis' commitment to organic farming and to the environment is almost unequalled – even in this book. For 27 years they have been breaking new ground and, while realising their ambition of creating a modern sustainable farm, they have shared their passions with their neighbours and their guests.

Giulia learned of the merits of organic farming from her parents – city-architect-turned-farmer father Augusto and her mother Adriana. In 1980, while living in Milan and running a tiny farm in Piedmont, Augusto and Adriana decided they should search for a bigger farm further into the countryside in Le Marche.

Northern Le Marche then was some way behind much of the rest of Italy and that attracted the Savinis. That the farm was within sight of Urbino delighted them, for being close to the city would add a cultural dimension to their new life.

"In the early 80s certified organic farming was in its infancy. Our beginning was not easy," says Giulia. "We lived in Milan while trying to oversee

the creation of a modern sustainable farm and of course the work and planning took a long time. Luckily Le Marche was some way ahead of the rest of Italy in organic farming although organic beef, that we planned to produce, was not easy to sell.

"We arrived with a deep respect for the soil – we didn't want to break the surface more than we had to – and we were regarded as townies who were nuts! The new machines we brought with us were seen as clear indications of our madness."

Undeterred they pressed on and are now respected for the dynamic farm they have created.

The Locanda stands among ancient, protected, oak trees. Its 1920s frame has grown into an unusual, unexpectedly modern, small hotel. The bigger rooms with the views are worth asking for.

During the renovation they double-insulated walls and roof, installed solar panels for heating water and have a wood-fired boiler that is fuelled with their own coppiced wood from their 185 acres of land. Loos have dual flushes, all light bulbs are low energy and bed linen is 100%

Locanda del Gallo

UMBRIA

Carved cockerels protect the doorways; indeed, they pop up everywhere. According to Balinese tradition, the cockerel – gallo – wards off evil spirits; numerous happy guests reckon he is doing a good job. Many of the models, in stone, papier maché, wood and steel have been given to Paola by guests as a token of appreciation for the peace and serenity they enjoyed during their stay. Her guest book bubbles over with thanks for the calm that emanates from this castle.

The castle is huge, its history is long and its battle scars many. High on a hill 'twixt the historically warring factions of Perugia and Gubbio, it could hardly escape. Paola, from Milan, and Irish, from Germany, have been here since 1997. A well-travelled cultured pair, they have injected a refreshing colonial mood into the old bones of the place. They have created seven exceptionally comfortable and stylish bedrooms

with limewashed walls, carved bedsteads, four-posters and marble bathrooms. There are heavy wooden reclaimed doors, friezes from Bali, carved mirrors, screens from India and Sri Lanka. Outside – there are grounds of 28 hectares – Indonesian furniture lines the verandahs, teak and canvas loungers loll about on the lawn, a wooden swing hangs from a tree.

Umbria is known as the green heart of Italy and the urge to explore it is not resistible. There are medieval hill-top towns as in its bejewelled neighbour, Tuscany, and Assisi, Orvieto, Gubbio, Perugia and Spello are all among Italy's most beautiful. The main squares in Todi and Assisi, like the squares in so many Umbrian towns, stand on the site of Roman forums.

Their churches are often as rich in art as galleries and many towns have remarkably well preserved Etruscan tombs. The lush Tiber valley

cuts through the province and, although there is no coastline, there are hugely popular lakes and lake 'beaches' for swimming.

Yogurt cake

3 cups yogurt
3 cups plain flour
1 cup sugar
3 eggs
1 cup sunflower oil
18g baking powder

• Mix all the ingredients together
• Grease a medium saverin cake tin (this is a doughnut-shaped tin with a hole in the centre so that you end up with a ring of cake)
• Cook at 180°C for 40 minutes
• Turn out, then dust with icing sugar to finish

Gubbio holds an annual Palio; unlike the furious horse race in Siena, this Palio is for runners only. Three teams devoted to Saints Ubaldo, Giorgio and Antonio set off around the cobbled streets in white trousers and red neckties. If you want to join in with the festival spirit, come on May 15. Spoleto's famous music festival, the Festival of Two Worlds, takes place annually during July.

Umbria's attractions and seductiveness may be enormous, but one is easily drawn back to the Locanda and its excellent restaurant (for guests only). The chef, Jimmy, is from Sri Lanka and for 14 years he has cooked imaginatively and with impressive flair, using vegetables and herbs from the garden. That he has been with the couple for so long – his wife, Kamani, is now part of the team, too – speaks volumes for the special atmosphere generated by Paola and Irish.

One of Paola's greatest pleasures is coming into contact with so many small local producers.

"There is no menu and we decide on the day what we will cook. Jimmy does the main meals and I look after the breads and cakes. We use as much of our own fresh produce as possible. The garden was wild when we came but Irish has carefully nurtured it. The land here is very dry but we choose plants that thrive in these conditions to minimise our need to water it – things such as rosemary and lavender and almond and olive trees.

"We enjoy creating dishes around the crops. For us a major part of Slow is about respecting foods available to us and, then, taking time to enjoy the finished dishes. Eating without stress is very important."

There are many courses held at the Locanda and there is a large and airy studio for dance or yoga. On request there is ayurvedic massage and, at a house nearby, Paola's friend Renza can teach guests the art of making pasta. "She is from Bologna and so very good!" (Note from Alastair: "Not unlikely: I ate my best lasagna ever in Bologna, though it was in 1968 I still remember it.") Renza, pictured at her loom, teaches weaving and natural dye, too.

Paola, a Milanese, is content in her adopted Umbria. "People have a good way of life here. It is unhurried and attention is given to food and sociability. I genuinely enjoy providing a place for people to unwind. Many of my guests lead stressful lives and I like to think that my work restores wellness."

Paola Moro & Irish Breuer

Locanda del Gallo,
loc. Santa Cristina, 06020 Gubbio
- 6 doubles, €120–€140. 3 suites for 4, €200–€240. Half-board €75–€90 p.p.
- Dinner €28. Lunch €12.
- +39 0759 229912
- www.locandadelgallo.it
- Train station: Perugia

Casa San Gabriel

UMBRIA

The seclusion, so high, will clear your head; the valley setting and the feeling of space create a deep sense of peace.

Neighbouring towns, such as Perugia, Gubbio, Cortona and Assisi, have the sort of multi-layered history that can startle the unwary. They tell you in Tuscany that Gubbio was one of the first five towns to be founded after the Flood.

"There is not a building, a stream, a tree, an odd-looking hillock or a strangely shaped field that was not the scene of some story." Thus wrote H V Morton. "The moment a peasant leaves his cottage he steps into a library of fiction for which a weekly newspaper seems a poor substitute."

From the house you can see the Basilica di San Francesco at Assisi perched at the bottom of Mount Subasio. But if the tranquility of Casa San Gabriel gets to you, you may want nothing but the simple pleasures of gathering a lettuce from the veg patch for lunch, watching the hoopoes foraging for their young, and snoozing under a tree.

Christina and David bought the Umbrian farm buildings in November 2002, began work the next February, got married

in August and opened, albeit in a low-key way, in October, less than a year after setting eyes on the ruin.

"We came here for peace and beauty, spurred on by our love of the Italian countryside and of the Italian people. Our lives here couldn't be more different: in London I was an accountant in a city firm, away from home 12 hours a day. I met David when I was working in Australia – he comes from Victoria – and decided that if we had a family I didn't want to do what I was doing; I would hardly have seen my children. We both wanted to carve out a life that put family at the centre."

Their two girls, Lucia and Elisabetta, are well-integrated – happily attending the little local school and nursery. Says Christina: "One of the things I relish is the introduction they have had to mealtimes as being happy, unrushed, shared occasions. Eli has a three-course lunch with her classmates and teachers. Everything served will be the sort of food that the cooks prepare for their families. It costs €4 a day; I think that is good value." Compare that to the budget given for English school lunches – 52p. What could better demonstrate the different approach to food taken by English and Italian governments.

The property is built on a 13th-century road and the main house dates back to the 16th century. It is said that Hannibal's army camped at the bottom of the valley next to the River Tiber that flows on from here and weaves its way right into Rome.

Wild Asparagus Risotto

500g (1lb) wild asparagus tips
2 onions/large shallots
olive oil
1 bottle Umbrian Grechetto or other dry white wine
2.5 cups risotto rice
vegetable stock
parmesan, freshly grated
handful chopped parsley

• Trim asparagus keeping only juicy bits. Add to boiling water and cook until tips are tender. Reserve drained liquid
• Heat veg stock. Sauté onions in oil until soft. Add rice and stir until shiny. Add 2 glasses of wine and stir until liquid has been absorbed. Add one ladleful of the hot asparagus water. Stir until absorbed
• Continue, adding small amounts of liquid each time. Add veg stock in same way. There is about 20 minutes of stirring to pour yourself a glass of wine. The rice is ready when it is cooked but still has bite
• Add the asparagus right at the end and sprinkle with parmesan and parsley to serve

They inflicted the worst defeat suffered by the Roman Empire at Lake Trasimeno, where they lured the Roman army into a narrow defile, so tight that the Romans couldn't properly wield their weapons, and slaughtered them. But Lake Trasimeno is beautiful, a vast watery oasis beside, and upon, which you can shake off the dust of a hot Umbrian summer.

Three farm buildings were converted for self-catering holidays and each has its own terrace. You feel part of something yet have privacy, too. David and Christina cook for guests on Tuesdays and on request can deliver three-course meals to each apartment for private suppers; on Thursday nights you can create your own pizza using the original bread oven and eat with everyone else in the garden. "David shops in Pierantonio for seasonal stuff; we pick wild asparagus and make good risottos and he will always pick up local wine for guests to try."

There is a small, cosy library with soft seats, and lots of books on travel and cookery and a table on the garden terrace for a group of friends to use. Magnificent views are at their best from the pool at the top of their land next to the little vineyard. You look down and may spot the girls pottering among the lettuces, David attempting to tame nature in the garden, Christina chatting to guests. The densely wooded valley seems to throw a cloak of silence around Casa San Gabriel.

"For us the beauty of a Slow life is having choice. We work hard but if we want to take the children to the lake for a sunny afternoon we can, and will maybe work in the evening instead. The children stay up late to join in with village life, festivals and fairs. 'How do they cope?' people always ask us. A siesta does the trick. We are always together," says Christina. "We do miss seeing friends and family regularly but I do know that we will never leave."

Christina Todd & David Lang

Casa San Gabriel, Vocablo Cal Zolari,
loc. Santa Giuliana 114, 06015 Pierantonio
- 3 apartments: 1 for 2, 1 for 2–4, 1 for 4.
  B&B: €85. Self-catering: €400–€1,025 per week.
- Dinner €25 (Tues); pizza €15 (Thurs).
- +39 0759 414219
- www.casasangabriel.com
- Train station: Perugia Pierantonio

Villa Aureli

UMBRIA

"Time has stood still here since 1700. There are plants, fine architecture, decoration, art and furniture from that period and many generations of our family have cared for Aureli."

Count Sperello di Serègo Alighieri's family arrived in 1874. Its members were doughty guardians who protected the estate and the wider community. Sperello's father saw off plans to build a motorway and to extend the village of Castel del Piano. During the war the house was occupied by Nazis, then by American, Australian and British troops but, thanks to the quick reaction of the faithful gardener Adolfo Guelfi who hid valuable possessions away behind false walls, remarkably little damage was done.

"Each generation has protected the house and the eco-system and we take pleasure in uniting our guests with our history," says Sperello. "We have installed photovoltaic panels to minimise energy usage, we illuminate gently and use much of our own produce."

Cleverly, water and energy usage have been cut without compromising on aesthetics. The small pool sits in the old rainwater reservoir and now

rainwater is harvested from the roofs and is used, along with water from the well, for the kitchen garden, the orangery and the fountain. The photovoltaic panels supply enough energy to aircondition two external apartments.

It is a productive estate and olive, lemon and orange trees are all nurtured without chemicals. The vegetable garden yields much produce and cook Adriana can create traditional Umbrian dishes for al fresco meals. The views are pretty enough to distract even the hungriest diner.

Within the formal gardens sit lemon trees in enormous 18th-century terracotta pots; the trees over-winter in the 'arancera' and, come spring, are taken to the garden by tractor. Sperello's father, Leonardo, remembered when it took 16 men to hoist them onto frames to transport them into position among the box and yews.

The 18th-century Italian colour schemes remain vivid and a special light permeates the villa. The proportions of the rooms are impressive yet its grandeur is not over-powering.

In the second half of the 18th century Sperello Aureli, an intellectual and art lover, slowly extended what had begun as a 16th-century tower; he added stucco-work and friezes and commissioned many of the fittings and much of the furniture. Sperello's grandmother, Anna Meniconi Bracceschi, whose parents bought the villa in 1874, loved this house and although she never lived here her gift was the magnificent tiling that was designed by her friend and crafted in Vietri near Naples.

There are four apartments – the two within the villa are majestic, one has four balconies and all have private access.

Sperello is an astrophysicist working at the Arcetri observatory in Florence; son Pietro, who studied philosophy, cares for things day-to-day. Pietro is a knowledgeable charming man, respectful and proud of all his family has preserved.

The jewels of Umbria are close by – the old centre of Perugia can be reached via train – and some of the great grapes of the wine world thrive on the slopes of Montefalco which translates to Falcon's Mount. The tourist authorities refer to it as 'la ringhiera dell'Umbria' – 'the balcony of Umbria' – and the views are worthy of the hyperbole.

Discover, too, the pleasures of Castel del Piano with its food stores and bars – perfect for an aperitif in the evening sun. Children will find contentment splashing in the pool, hiding in the garden or visiting the sheep, hens, cat and dog.

If you need to stay in touch, you can at least do it Italian style in the garden under the 'internet' tree in the company of the bees and the birds.

Sperello di Serègo Alighieri

Villa Aureli,
via Luigi Cirenei 70, 06132 Castel del Piano
- 4 apartments: 1 for 4, 1 for 4–8, 1 for 6, 1 for 5. €700–€1,500 per week.
- Occasional dinner with wine, €36. Restaurant 2km.
- +39 340 6459061
- www.villaaureli.it
- Train station: Perugia

La Palazzetta del Vescovo

UMBRIA

Polished perfection and professionalism run through the veins of La Palazzetta. Its owners are a delightful couple that fled the strains of their careers in marketing to reconnect with people – and to gather a little serenity.

They brought considerable skills from their former life – not least their languages: French, English and Spanish – and gently transplanted them to great effect here in Umbria. The house is beautiful, a magnet for visitors, and so is the food. They take huge pride in what they have done and it is fun as a visitor to be immersed in it all. "We did not move to make money," says Stefano. "We came to reclaim ourselves, to make the sort of connections with people and nature that are difficult to forge in corporate life when you are rushed and stressed." To further their aim of reducing stress in their guests, there is massage available in the old cellars, an easy-going labrador called Chiaretta, wine-tastings in the *cantina* and every possible inducement to slow down and relax.

Here only the bells from a nearby convent or the hum of the tractor will disturb your thoughts. The 18th-century

hilltop Palazzetta – once a summer residence for the bishops of Todi, utterly abandoned in the 1960s – was bought by Paola and Stefano in 2000.

They began the restoration in 2004 and by 2006 had created four cool, elegant sitting rooms and nine lovely bedrooms in subtle, muted colours. Some have muslin-draped four-posters, some have antiques gathered from Naples, some hand-painted cupboards and bedside tables. They are all beautifully furnished but unpretentious – not an unusual Italian achievement. Even the fabrics are delightful: handmade covers on the beds, fluffy towels and bathrobes, and Quagliotti linen sheets.

Everything about the house seems generous. To add to all this, each room has a head-clearing view over steeply falling vineyards and the Tiber valley. Stupendous! On a clear day you can see as far as Perugia. The newly-planted gardens, the terrace and the infinity pool give you those same, ineffable, views.

Paola's mother is Umbrian and family connections drew them here, as did the authenticity (their word) of the region. "Umbria is not geared around tourists in the way that Tuscany can be. No doubt Tuscany is beautiful but sometimes it can feel too busy, busy with tourists who make little connection with real rural activity," says Stefano.

Paola is a patron chef with considerable flair, taking organic, local ingredients and traditional recipes then adding her own twist with unexpected flavours and combinations of ingredients. She and Stefano, a sommelier, respect the Slow Food Movement for protecting artisan food producers who hold out against EU hygiene regulations. "Take Lardo di Colonnata. It has been made for centuries in northern Tuscany by putting the pork belly fat in a marble sink with salt and spices and leaving it for six months. It is part of Italy's culture and identity," asserts Stefano, "but suddenly it was not going to be allowed because of health fears. The Slow Food Movement awarded it a Presidio status and has saved it from being banned."

Stefano and Paola have done a lot to reduce the environmental impact of their business. There are automatic light sensors, water butts, careful policy on laundering towels, and they have not only reused old materials in the renovation but have used furnishings made with natural fibres.

The time they have clawed back for themselves has, then, been put to a greater good. "We take time over important things and being with people is our greatest reward. We spend time with people in their best moments and a big part of our salary is the sheer fun."

Paola Maria & Stefano Zocchi

La Palazzetta del Vescovo,
via Clausura 17, Fr. Spineta, 06054 Fratta Todina

- 9 doubles, €180–€260. Singles €125–€180.
- Lunch, on request, €15-€25, . Dinner, 4 courses, €40.
- +39 0758 745183
- www.lapalazzettadelvescovo.com
- Train station: Marsciano

I Mandorli Agriturismo

UMBRIA

Wanda, mother and grandmother, is the overseer of this 45-hectare estate. With her three daughters, Maria, Alessandra and Sara, and their daughters, you have the privilege of seeing Italian family life in action.

I Mandorli is a higgledy-piggledy house with little steps here and there leading to rooms and apartments, outhouses, lofts, old olive mills. Flowers tumble from pots, capers scale stone walls and fruit and cypress trees give shade in the garden. Bedrooms are sweet, simple affairs with new wrought-iron beds and pale homemade patchwork quilts; the small bathrooms are spotless.

The vineyard is managed organically; vegetables and sunflowers are grown and there is a little outlet for the estate's produce; you can buy wine, lentils, oils and jams to take home. Sara says "Guests can relax into our lives here, wander on our land, pick herbs, help with the olive harvest, take cookery lessons, cycle, walk and go rafting. Children will love the wooden slide and seesaw, the old pathways and steps on this shallow hillside, the new pool

– wonderful to return to after outings to Assisi and Spoleto.

Umbria is rich in festivals, too, particularly in October. There are solemn processions honouring patron saints in January, a jollier San Feliciano feast day on 24 January, a San Emiliano feast day on 28 January, and in October a medieval fayre in Trevi. You can visit the oldest olive tree in Umbria just across the road or go to Assisi to see Giotto's frescoes in the basilica; it is hard to know in which direction to head first.

The family understands that most guests lead lives more stressful than they would wish. Sara speaks with poetic eloquence: "For people in every corner of the world, work is characterised by stress, deadlines and daily battles. We want people to stop, to enjoy a moment of peace. It is essential to their spiritual well-being. We want to give our guests space to experience these moments.

"We are lucky that our family has been so deeply rooted in the countryside, living among the olive trees for more than three centuries. Our culture here is born from a deep respect for everything that nature offers us. The unexpected death of our father was a great shock. When we were little we used to follow him as he worked on the farm, in the countryside and woodland. He would always stop to explain what he was doing – and why. After school we'd head for the olive groves to meet the women who harvested the fruit. They would sing and chant as they worked, and tell us stories. These beautiful memories, and many more, made us carry on with it all when he died. It is our passion and we want to continue his good work."

The whole family speaks of the bond between man and nature, the need to value the earth not just as a producer but as a creator of tradition. The idea of agriturism is to unite guests with family traditions and regional stories and history. The Zappelli Cardarellis remain faithful to the philosophy.

I Mandorli is aptly named: there's at least one almond tree outside each apartment. The blossom in February is stunning and, in summer, masses of greenery shades the old *casa padronale*.

Each daughter speaks a different foreign language, so nobody is excluded from the conviviality of the house. Guests are helped with their itineraries and the sisters promote walking and biking – even if just through the olive groves, for there are over 5,000 of them.

"We believe the pivotal thing here, in this sea of green that surrounds us, is that each person who comes can find a different way of being."

Famiglia di Zappelli Cardarelli

I Mandorli Agriturismo,
loc. Fondaccio 6, fraz. Bovara, 06039 Trevi
- 1 twin/double, 2 triples. €40–€85.
  3 apartments: 1 for 2, 2 for 4. €65–€150.
- Restaurant 800m.
- +39 0742 78669
- www.agriturismoimandorli.com
- Train station: Trevi 3km; Foligno 15km

La Torretta

LAZIO

"Slow has been the story of our lives." So says Maureen Scheda, speaking for herself and for her architect husband Roberto.

Maureen had, like many of us, a red-hot passion for Italy, its history, language and art. Unlike many of us, she moved to Italy to embrace all that she held dear. In the 60s she left Wales for Rome, met Roberto and married him in '68. But after having two children, Rome was not Slow enough and Maureen's thoughts were turning to the idea of living in a medieval hill-top village.

They gave up lucrative careers and plumped for a move to Casperia – a higgledy-piggledy joyful, vibrant village perched in the Sabine hills. Maureen opened a small craft shop where she sold wooden dolls and the woollen clothes she made on her own loom. In the workshop next door, Roberto designed and made wooden furniture. Meanwhile, their search for a family house had begun and soon after

their arrival in Casperia, they found their dream home in La Torretta. The 15th-century, dilapidated, palazzo was waiting to be rescued from dereliction and this talented, visionary pair were ready.

Roberto poured his heart, soul and architectural talent into its restoration. "He used skilled local labour, he made furniture and even, one sweltering summer, 20 huge solid doors," remembers Maureen. "We kept all material and work faithful to the period."

It is a stunning, lofty house with dreamy views and beautiful interior spaces, such as: a huge, ground-floor sitting room with frescoes around the cornice, a giant fireplace, modern sofas and chairs, books, paintings and piano. The upper room, where meals are taken, is a stunning, vaulted, contemporary space with an impressive kitchen of Carrara marble and views through skylights to the church tower and valley. The terrace views are spectacular.

Pasta alla Rocca

3 onions, chopped
75g (3oz) butter
2 large yellow peppers, puréed
1 cup water
150g (6oz) gorgonzola cheese, crumbled
splash of cream
small handful parmesan cheese
500g (1lb) Farfalle pasta
parsley, chopped, and pepper to garnish

• Melt butter in a large pan, fry onions until soft
• Add puréed peppers, stir and cover and cook until soft and thickened for about 40 minutes. Add a little water if dry
• Add gorgonzola and cream and leave on low heat while you cook the pasta
• Add pasta to sauce, toss and serve topped with parmesan, parsley and pepper

Step out and you will understand why German historian Gregorovius wrote in *Wandering in Italy* "In all my travels I've never beheld a panorama of such heroic beauty."

Maureen had, quietly, another ambition. "Our goal was that our work would help to revitalise the village. So many people were seeking work in the cities, abandoning their beautiful birthplaces for a humdrum life of commuting. We wanted to show them what treasures they had right here in Casperia, that it could be possible to live and work in the village."

Her hunch was that if the Casperia villagers embraced their birthplace then tourists looking for a 'real' Italy would be drawn there.

"I wanted to do what I could to attract visitors. I worked in tourism after moving here and became a tour director. We have battled with local authorities to preserve the environment and the identity of the village. We have made progress and

Casperia now knows a little tourism. Other bed and breakfasts run by local people have opened, there

"Our goal was that our work would help revitalise the village"

are three restaurants, a yoga retreat and an ever-growing interest in Slow food.

"We have been a member of the Slow Food Movement since it started and now have our own leader in Casperia and 26 members. I did a programme with the BBC's Countryfile programme introducing the conviviums and their work here."

Maureen and Roberto organise walking holidays and climbing holidays, too – one of her daughters is a qualified instructor and the other runs cookery courses. Their local Slow food expert organises wine and olive oil tastings and they have hosted international voluntary workers

striving to keep open the local 'no asphalt' walking paths.

Maureen and Roberto would get a medal from us if we had one. Expatriates are so often out of tune with their communities, bringing in alien ideas and subtly undermining traditions. But Maureen, with Roberto's support, has sailed her little ship into battle with the invading world of Fast with the vigour and determination, let alone the panache, of a whole fleet.

Roberto & Maureen Scheda

La Torretta,
via G. Mazzini 7, 02041 Casperia
- 5 doubles, €90. 1 single, €70.
  2 connecting rooms for a family, €150.
- Dinner with wine €30, by arrangement.
- +39 0765 63202
- www.latorrettabandb.com
- Train station: Poggio Mirteto

Campania

Basilicata

Puglia

Sicily & Aeolian Islands

[THE SOUTH]

[THE SOUTH]

Southern Italy is a country apart; it saw the flowering of the ancient Greek colonies - the Magna Grecia - and was home to great philosophers, moralists, mathematicians and scientists. Later the Romans took over, then northern European tribes. Then Islamic, Norman and Byzantine invaders came, stayed and went, each bringing their culture, their learning and their style of architecture.

From the 14th century until Italy was unified in 1860, southern Italy was known as 'The Kingdom of the Two Sicilies'; the combined kingdoms of Naples and Sicily. Naples was the capital and Palermo the second city. At different times Aragonese, Angevin, Bourbon and Bonaparte dynasties all held the strings and left their mark.

The south is not new to tourism. The English gentry on their Grand Tours loved staying in Venice, Florence and Rome but the hospitality they loved best was found in Naples and Sicily; gastronomic and cultural encounters with their hosts there were enjoyed as much as the architectural gems of the rest of the country.

Each region has its own character but shares the same palette: the gold of durum wheat, the white peaks of craggy mountains, the silver of a shimmering sea and of olive leaves, the rich hues of fertile earth burnished by the rawness of the southern sun.

Seafood, mountain lamb and goat are easy to find, and the wild herbs and vegetables grown in small-holdings are artfully used with each. The olive oil and wine are exceptional. This is a land that has known hard times and its now-famous cuisine - particularly in Puglia - has always used whatever the climate and land has allowed. Homemade bread and pasta are fragrant and delicious; it seems there is a home-rolled pasta shape for every day of the year. The region's

"southern Italy is striding into the future with confidence"

cheeses - *burrata, mozzarella, scamorza, manteca, provola, caciocavallo* - are famous worldwide.

No one has tasted a real pizza, nor *mozzarella di bufala*, until they have been to Napoli, nor savoured a tomato until they have bitten into a *Pomodoro San Marzano*. **Campania** is the home of the people's dish, *spaghetti al pomodoro*. It is also the home of the courtly *timballo di maccheroni*, the *sartu' di riso* and the Lacryma *cristi del vesuvio* wine.

See the jewels of the Amalfi coast from a new perspective, from the 'steps of the Gods'. Well-signed shepherds' paths run between Amalfi, Positano and Equense, winding through lemon groves and bee hives and past smallholders working the land. The classical music of the Ravello Music Festival is performed against unforgettable backdrops.

Puglia is neighbour to Campania and there are only 130 miles between the Adriatic and Tyrrhenian Seas here. The National Park of Gargano is a promontory that juts out into the Adriatic. You'll find myriad flora, a vertiginous coastline and coastal land bars that separate the lakes of Lesina and Varano from the Adriatic. The Foresta Umbra is a rare example of a pre-historic Mediterranean landscape. The area also has the Parco Eolico dell'Alberone, one of the largest alternative energy plants in Europe.

The spiritual life of the south is legendary and all saints are celebrated with extraordinary displays of devotion, parades and feasting. The **Basilicata** landscape is animated with places of worship - pagan and profound - built over the millennia. The pre-historic Sassi of Matera, now a World Heritage site, is where Benedictine and Greek monks once lived in caves and churches carved out of the rock. Genoese architect Renzo Piano, who co-designed the Pompidou Centre in Paris, has designed a cathedral in local stone to honour one of the Catholic church's most recent saints, Padre Pio. Some say it is the most popular and striking pilgrimage shrine ever built.

There is a growing literary scene in Matera inspired by Isabella Morra, a poet and one of the few female voices from the Renaissance. Author Carlo Levi lived at Aliano and his home is now a museum of rural life; in his book *Christ Stopped at Eboli,* he described the tragedy of the south in the 1930s at the time of the mass migrations.

The recipes of Basilicata often include chilli, goat's cheese, pork sausages dried and preserved in olive oil, and *lampascioni*, wild onions. The finest wine is Aglianico del Vulture, from grapes grown on volcanic slopes; Malvasia del Vulture is a straw-coloured slightly sweet wine.

In Palermo in **Sicily**, seven days a week, you will encounter thriving markets as vibrant as any souk. Try some *panelle rici'ciri*, chickpea fritters, as you lose yourself in the maze. On Sunday take a train to its seaside satellite and lunch with the locals; crack open *ricci* (sea urchins) and taste the sea. Check out the *pasticceria* and the *gelati con panna* (they claim that ice-cream was invented here).

Disappear into the mountains from Siracusa and explore the Pantalica gorge on foot or take a trek on horseback. In June, immerse yourself in the Classical Greek Theatre Festival in the ruins.

The south is scattered with small towns animated by traditions and by people who respect the food they produce and who have a powerful sense of belonging. Don't be fooled into thinking that you have stepped back into another era; southern Italy is treasuring its history, yet striding into the future with confidence.

Lindy Wildsmith

THE SOUTH

ROME

Lago di Lesina
Lago di Varano
San Severo
Manfredonia
Fòggia
Cerignola
Barletta
Trani
Andria
Canosa di Puglia
Ofanto
202
Bitonto
Bari
PUGLIA
Monopoli
206
Fasano
214
Gravina in Puglia
Altamura
Ostuni
210
Martina Franca
Brindisi
Matera
Grottaglie
Mesagne
Massafra
Francavilla Fontana
Taranto
Manduria
Lecce
Copertino
Nardò
Galatina
Gallipoli

Caserta
Benevento
CAMPANIA
Avellino
NAPLES
Isola d'Ischia
Torre Annunziata
Nocera Inferiore
Isola Ventotene
Castellammare di Stabia
Salerno
198
Sorrento
Battipaglia
Potenza
Coglian
Isola di Capri
Tanagro
BASILICATA
Agri
218
Parco Nazionale Del Pollino

Split
Dubrovnik
Corfu
Corfu

Adriatic
Sea

Golfo di Taranto

Cosenza

CALABRIA

Tyrrhenian Sea

Aeolian Islands
226 *I. Salina*

Vibo Valentia

Capo di Milazzo
Milazzo
Messina
Barcellona
Reggio di Calabria

N

Capo S. Vito
PALERMO
Cefalù
Monti Nebrodi
Monti Peloritani
222 Taormina
Tràpani
Alcamo
Monte Etna
Marsala
Castelvetrano
Monti Sicani
Paternò
Acireale
Mazara del Vallo
SICILY
Enna
Sciacca
Caltanissetta
✈ **Catania**
Agrigento
Lentini
Ionian Sea
Caltagirone
Augusta
Licata
Gela
Syracuse
Vittòria
Ragusa
Mòdica
Capo Pàssero

0 20 40 60 80 100 kilometres
0   20   40   60 miles

Special places to stay

Campania

 198 Azienda Agricola Le Tore

Puglia

202 Lama di Luna – Biomasseria

206 Masseria Serra dell'Isola

210 Masseria Il Frantoio

214 Masseria Impisi

Basilicata

 218 San Teodoro Nuovo Agriturismo

Sicily & Aeolian Islands

222 Hotel Villa Schuler

226 Hotel Signum

Azienda Agricola Le Tore

CAMPANIA

For over 200 years, oils and wines have flowed from Le Tore. When Vittoria took over the 18th-century farm 25 years ago she reinvigorated not only the land but, it seems, the whole community. With the help of locals she renovated buildings, planted lemon and olive groves, orchards and vegetable gardens, created a dining room from the old cantina and made generous bedrooms from high-ceilinged – Volte Sorrentine – rooms. Antonio, one of her helpers, has been with her for 26 years, tending the crops, propping up the fruit trees, putting the land to rest in autumn and managing heroically when things spring to life after winter. He manages the small weekly market, too; Le Tore has such abundant produce that they sell to local families and restaurateurs.

Vittoria is eloquent on the subject of agritourism for which Italy is famous – and for which she is qualified to speak, for she is President of the Associazione Nazionale per l'Agriturismo.

"Much of Europe has rural tourism but in Italy the association between accommodation and farming is especially close. If during your stay on an agriturismo you can't see farm work, you can be sure that it is happening somewhere; maybe grain is being processed off-site or grapes will have already been sent for pressing locally. Always, the owner will be connected to the land and will have a real desire to bring the guest closer to the activity of the rural community."

"Local agriturismi work well together, too. Between us we find everyone a bed," says Vittoria. "At certain times of year those of us who grow the same crops can't cope with B&B, so farmers who are growing different crops lend us a hand and take in guests. Then we reverse roles at their harvest time." It is an harmonious environment in which to live, work or run a business, one in which work and

pleasure are more closely intertwined than in urban areas. Working around people's talents and

> "In agriturismi, the owners are connected to the land and have a real desire to bring the guest closer to the rural community"

needs means that much can be achieved. "With a spirit of collaboration so much more is possible," says Vittoria wisely.

You can see, at the many festivals, the reverence given to farm produce. There is the Palm Sunday Carnival that celebrates pigs, for example, and there are fairs around the vendemmia (grape) and apple harvests. Many Italian farms, 15%-20%, are certified as organic and there is a high concentration of organic farms in Southern Italy. Many of them are small-scale and have benefited

from hilly sites: the breezes reduce the incidence of disease and pests. The main production on this AIAB (Italian Association for Biological Agriculture)-certified farm is olive oil and Vittoria's newest customers are the Japanese. "It's not only the oils that they like, but everything needed to make pizza and even pizza ovens. We sell 1,000 bottles of oil a year to Japan."

You can sample all these wonderful ingredients dining with other guests and taking your aperitifs together in the courtyard. Among other specialities, you are likely to have purée of broad bean with chicory, calamari salad, marinated anchovies, grilled home-grown vegetables with their own lemon Ovale di Sorrento. Vittoria is usually there and is worth quizzing if you are planning to explore. She did a thesis on the micro-climate of the Amalfi coast so knows almost every inch, its beaches, flora, fauna and undiscovered corners. She can point you to paths such as the

CAI-marked Alta Via di Lattari that runs along the southern side of the peninsular.

Le Tore is 500 metres above sea level and on the crest of the hill of Sant'Agata sui Due Golfi that divides the sunny dry gulf of Amalfi from the greener and more humid Gulf of Sorrento. You can drop down to coast level – around 15 minutes' drive, one hour's walk – for boats to Capri, Ischia and Naples; Pompeii, Ercolano and Oplonti are 45 minutes by train from Sorrento.

It is refreshing to find a place like Le Tore in an area that, down at sea level, is more known for its swish bars, its sailing fraternity, and 'smart' coastline that seduces international travellers. Here you are in touch with the people who help to sustain the local economy, providing wonderful produce for many of those bars and restaurants.

Vittoria is a dynamic, busy lady who is, quite properly, more interested in agriculture than in tourism. But she takes pride in all she does, so

sweeping travellers into her daily embrace is natural for her. One guest said: "What a joy to spend time at such an authentic place. Vittoria, ever kind, even gave us an Italian cooking lesson before dinner."

This passion for good food is, of course, at the heart of the Slow movement – a bright light at the end of the dark tunnel of fast and lifeless food that is doing so much to tear our communities apart. Italy, with all its Vittorias, is leading the way.

Signora Vittoria Brancaccio

Azienda Agricola Le Tore, via Pontone 43, Sant'Agata sui Due Golfi, 80064 Massa Lubrense
- 4 doubles, 1 twin, 1 family room. €90. 1 apartment for 5, €700–€1,000 per week.
- Dinner €25, by arrangement. Restaurant 5-min walk.
- +39 0818 080637
- www.letore.com
- Train station: Sorrento

Lama di Luna Biomasseria

PUGLIA

Forty-four families once lived in this substantial dwelling in Murgia, and the place still has the feel of a centre for the wider community. The extended families lived around the courtyard with the bread oven in the centre – an efficient way of sharing resources and bringing people together over a common activity.

When Pietro bought the place in 1990 he had no idea that his grandmother's sister had sold it out of the family in 1820, so he had, through pure and delightful chance, done the proper thing by bringing it back into the family. He immediately ousted errant sheep and began to treat the land with deep respect.

It is a most handsome and traditional farm that began in the 17th century and, after years of neglect, is going strong again. Pietro claims that it is the most perfectly integrated organic farm in Italy, and it may well be, with his passion for the environment and his respect for tradition and craftsmanship reaching into every crevice.

Shapes are rounded, there is nothing chemical in the rooms, no dyes, no bleaches; the beds are positioned north to south to ensure more peaceful sleep; each bedroom has its own fireplace – and once housed an entire family! Guests now also have a library to retreat to and a generous veranda for sunset and star-gazing.

Pietro has created his own laundry to avoid the chemicals used by outside laundries. Tiles, and even basins, are made by hand and to traditional methods; bed linen is unbleached, mattresses are of natural latex and tablecloths and curtains are of hessian; the walls have been lime-washed rather than painted, the furniture polished with linseed oil; reclaimed wood has been used for doors and the food, of course, is devotedly organic.

Masseria Serra dell'Isola

PUGLIA

The old masseria may not immediately bewitch you but its interior and its history will. With Rita's warmth, humour, pride and gift for animatedly recounting her family's history, it will all prove impossible to resist.

"I open my home out of a love for Puglia. My great pleasure is to lead those who come to visit towards paths and scenery that are rarely seen. My descriptions, in the words of someone who has spent her life here, are my gifts to my guests. In our agricultural civilisation, giving is not an indefinite and anonymous exchange of presents, it means sharing something precious. Sharing is the foundation of this society and in a world that spins around the individual, we should rediscover the genuine joy of it."

What a delightful way of articulating her way of being. It is thanks to passionate Puglians like Rita that it is such a privilege to learn more about these lesser-known areas, their customs, traditions, food and people. She and her fellow Puglians are doing a grand job: southern cuisine has a growing army of fans, as do the area's Truilli houses, coastline and archaeological riches.

Rita eloquently describes the history of the Norman, Swabian and Angevin castles in Bari, the Romanesque cathedrals and medieval villages like Polignano and Monopoli. "Outside the whitewashed walls of my masseria I introduce my guests to the things so easily missed by the hurried tourist."

Her 17th-century masseria is well worth getting to know too. Built by her ancestors in 1726 as an olive mill and summer residence, the house has an impressive library of books on history, art and cookery. Rita has hand-written recipes from her great grandmother's kitchen,

recipes that she still uses for rosoli (liquors), jams, and cakes; she will happily share them with you.

The great hall has uneven stone floors and once housed the olive mill. It is, like the rest of the house, filled with portraits and antiques. The light, gracious bedrooms are named after the women who once occupied them – Donnas Angelina, Ritella, Annina – and the elegant old beds bear fine new mattresses.

Rita explains a little of her previous life: "I studied law as a student, then I became a journalist working on a daily newspaper. I reported on environmental and agricultural issues and then worked for the International Center for Advanced Mediterranean Agronomic Studies. Now I am working with Bari University, helping them with research into natural fertilisers for our land."

In 1992 she was awarded a prize for her outstanding environmental essays. "Now I dedicate myself to the study of Puglia's history," she

Cartellate (Christmas pastries)

For the dough:
330g (13oz) flour
70g (2.5oz) olive oil
half teaspoon salt

For glazing and decoration:
500g (1lb) honey or half litre vincotto (grape syrup)
1 glass of water or white wine
caster sugar
ground cinnamon

• Mix flour, oil and salt into a dough and roll out very thinly. Cut into 15-cm long finger-width strips. Curl each strip to form a rose shape (use your imagination!). Fry roses in a little olive oil
• Warm up the honey or the vincotto then add the water/white wine. Bring to boil. Dunk the roses into the syrup, dust with sugar and cinnamon. Serve cold.

explains, "and the southern Italian identity, and I am also writing a travel guide."

Puglia, curiously, was ruled by the Byzantines for over two centuries and flowered magnificently under the Hohenstaufen Emperors. In the 13th century, under Frederic II, palaces and cathedrals were built on a grand scale, but Puglia went into a long decline thereafter and knew only rule by other foreigners, slave raids on the coast, and growing poverty. It was not until 1860, when she became part of the new Italian nation, that things began to look up. They are looking better than ever right now, with tourism giving the region a much-needed lift.

It is an honour, then, if Rita is available, to have her guide you personally through markets, historic sites, cookery lessons. Her food is all home-made, from produce mostly grown here and accompanied by local wines. There is a real spirit of conviviality when the house is full and everyone gathers in the beautiful dining room. "I consider myself the guardian of a tradition and of a place where time and the frenetic rhythm of the metropolis are far away. The masseria isn't a character in search of an author or an ethereal mansion. It is a part of history and here it seems that time stopped centuries ago."

If you want to go slowly, it would be hard to begin at a better place.

Rita Guastamacchia

Masseria Serra dell'Isola,
S.P.165 Mola, Conversano n.35, 70042 Mola di Bari
- 4 doubles, 2 twins/doubles, €130.
  Whole house €3,300-€3,900 per week.
- Dinner, 3 courses, €35-€40. Wine €12-€18.
- +39 349 5311256 (mobile)
- www.masseriaserradellisola.it
- Train station: Mola di Bari, 4km

Masseria Il Frantoio

PUGLIA

"This corner of our world is rich in a deep and simple charm. The distances between villages are small; the countryside is peppered with vineyards, dry stone walls and white walled houses. It has a magic of its own."

That is Armando describing the delights of Puglia, down in the hot southern heel of Italy and a fascinating landscape of mountains, plains, beaches and forests. Invaded and occupied numerous times, like most of Italy, it can draw upon a glittering array of cultural influences. Nearby Ostuni seems as Arabic as it is Italian. With its whitewashed houses and walls, it is known as 'La Citta Bianca'.

Il Frantoio is much loved for its food, especially for the eight-course meal that is a showcase for southern Italian cooking. Turn up during dinner and you may feel you have stumbled onto a film set: the courtyard twinkles with candles and sparkling glasses, music drifts from the house, Armando glides elegantly between the tables explaining the provenance and flavours of each little dish and of the wines he has chosen for you.

The masseria runs on well-oiled wheels, with each family member assigned a role that draws on their strengths. Daughter Serenella works alongside her husband Silvio and helper Giuseppe to look after the 72 hectares of olive groves and orchards; Armando looks after the staff, sources the wine and is very much 'front of house'; Rosalba has worked magic within the house and the kitchens.

The farmhouse is centred on a 16th-century olive press; parts of it were built in 1544 and the 10 bedrooms are in the 19th-century part of the house. The visitors' quarter is a series of beautiful rooms, ranging from fairytale with lace and toile to formal with antique armoires and gilt-framed art. It is a gloriously eclectic mix. Despite the

professional edge to this dynamic masseria, the homely touches are ever-present; linen and towels are washed in organic soap and line-dried. There is a kitchen for guests to use, sitting rooms and a library. The 16th-century citrus garden, with lemon, orange and mandarin trees and the odd peacock, is alive with colours and fragrances.

From the kitchen garden, nurtured by Abele, come vegetables, herbs and edible flowers. Rosalba

> "We conduct ourselves in a way that is at one with nature. Guests say what we are doing is special but we are simply behaving in a way that should be normal for everybody"

oversees the menus and she and her six chefs create elaborate flavours with simple ingredients; a different olive oil is used in each of the eight courses. "We reproduce centuries-old local recipes; food in the south comes from a long history of peasant dishes," explains Armando. "Specialists worldwide have recognised the diet of Puglia as a healthy one. It goes without saying that we work with seasonal produce."

They also make liquor, jams, pickles, preserves and pâtés to ensure that none of their crops go to waste; you can buy jars to take home. Armando and his helpers can guide you around the cellars and explain the workings of the impressive olive press. Rosalba's collection of antique christening robes and fabrics are on show, too. The library has over 1500 books rescued from the cellars and each has been cleaned and restored.

The masseria is almost a world in itself. But it is very much part of Puglia and that special landscape. The lush Itrian Valley is rich in archaeological sites. Seven kilometres away are the

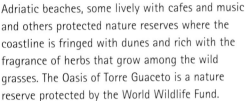

Adriatic beaches, some lively with cafes and music and others protected nature reserves where the coastline is fringed with dunes and rich with the fragrance of herbs that grow among the wild grasses. The Oasis of Torre Guaceto is a nature reserve protected by the World Wildlife Fund.

There is a palpable sense of contentment among all who work at Frantoio. Staff are treated as if they were family, which creates a lovely atmosphere. Giuseppe is the olive expert and seems to know each tree; Thea and Lilly provide breakfast and bake the cakes; Silvana welcomes you and looks after the practicalities of your stay. The passion of the Balestrazzi couple is infectious and you cannot fail to be touched by their respect for nature, the history of the area and of the house.

Armando and Rosalba see themselves as guardians of the impressive masseria, judiciously mixing modern and traditional ideas. Armando refers to his olive trees as the 'patrons' of the old masseria. "Thanks to these great veterans, some of which are the oldest and largest of their kind, we can carry on producing our exceptional extra virgin olive oil." A farmer with less sensitivity might well chop them down and replant with more 'efficient' trees.

"We conduct ourselves in a way that is at one with nature. Guests say that what we are doing is special but we say that we are simply behaving in a way that should be normal for everybody."

Silvana Caramia

Masseria Il Frantoio,
SS 16km 874, 72017 Ostuni
- 3 doubles, 2 triples, 3 family rooms. €176–€220.
  Apartment for 2–4, €319–€350.
- Dinner with wine, €55, by arrangement.
- +39 0831 330276
- www.masseriailfrantoio.it
- Train station: Ostuni

Masseria Impisi

PUGLIA

You may know Masseria Impisi from Channel 4's Grand Designs programme: Kevin McCloud came to witness its renovation by the enterprising David and Leonie and was blown away by what they had achieved. This likeable pair of artists took an abandoned olive farm, with tumble-down cattle stalls and, under the scrutiny of television cameras and on a budget of £19,000, created a Romanesque colonnaded house that is hard to resist.

On that budget David and Leonie's only choice was to do the work themselves. Their back-breaking efforts and wide-ranging artistic talents combined to create something so remarkable that they were inundated with requests from people wanting to take part in one of their 'Il Collegio' holidays, or just to stay and see for themselves the finished masseria.

They were in danger of becoming victims – albeit happy ones – of their own success. It wasn't easy looking after as many as 14 guests, cooking three meals a day, helping them in their artwork or touring around Puglia with them was demanding.

"We were incredibly busy after the programme," says

David. "We had been offering this sort of holiday for 16 years so our experience carried us through but it couldn't last. We had promised ourselves that we would run a business, not let it run us."

So, they did what we all dream of doing; they stepped back and took a long, hard look at their lives.

"We change what we do every year. Demand was still there for the courses but we wanted to punctuate the year with pauses to enjoy our home and explore new things. We wanted, too, to get back in touch with our lives as artists, to do more experimental work."

Leonie, who did the intricate mosaic work around the masseria, is a professional painter, was a lecturer at Falmouth College of Art and has held Artist in Residence posts. Her interest is Medieval and Early Renaissance art. David, who has made furniture and created carvings for their Italian home, graduated from Falmouth then did post-graduate studies in drawing and sculpture at the Slade School of Art. No wonder they were able to create a place of such beauty.

After much soul-searching, they decided to offer just two

or three courses a year, though artists who are happy to operate under their own steam can still use the studio facilities. People can choose to do b&b or to self-cater and David and Leonie can organise sailing, snorkeling and riding. The Via Triana Cycle Trail follows the old roman road along the coast and you can set off on the Masseria's free bikes. The couple's past experience of organising art and gastronomic holidays means they have stacks of useful local advice.

They have created one apartment for two in a 15th-century gatehouse, one further apartment for two and have two more double rooms. They have hosted weddings – their olive mill room can take up to 40 people – and will take care of the legalities of marriage and help in many practical ways.

Their gardens are a lush oasis among the olive plains. They are in a tiny valley and are watered by their own well and harvested grey water. Among it all, flanked by Leonie's mosaics, is a pool hewn from the limestone rock. They are working on a little eco-dwelling to house the young students who come to help keep the grounds and the house looking so lovely.

David and Leonie are delighted that Puglia is finally being recognised: its reputation as a destination for foodies is well-earned and growing and its Slow credentials are impressive. It is largely a self-sustaining community, too, as so much produce is grown here.

"The locals were helped by the European Agricultural Policy that dished out subsidies in the 60s and 70s to lift market gardens out of their moribund state. A quarter of Europe's wine is produced here and oil from the olive groves around Brindisi was among the first to be granted DOP (denomination of protected origin) status by the Italian ministry of agriculture. "Puglian farmers used to export their best produce, now they keep it here for themselves. And it is impossible to eat badly. Food is beautifully cooked and presented, and it is

great value. The number of restaurants with Slow Food status is growing apace."

Traditionally there has been a divide in Italy between Northern Italians and Southern. The south has been economically repressed while the rich north prospered on the back of big industry and cheap southern labour. But we are beginning to value natural wealth, particularly in times of economic turmoil and rising fuel prices.

"Northerners can be very rude about the Southerners. But the people here are rooted in the earth, they have used every patch of land to grow something, and the quality of their wine, oil and fresh produce is now acknowledged. Much of what is produced has been organic; they simply couldn't afford the fertilisers. The bulk of our food comes from within a 10-mile radius and the low transport costs make it far cheaper than elsewhere.

"There is an old-fashioned courtesy, too. If you ask someone directions to a restaurant, they are likely to walk you there. They feel duty-bound to look after visitors."

Ostuni has applied for World Heritage status and generally, David says, the South's self-respect is growing. It can compete on many fronts and is gathering respect worldwide. "Untangling all the threads of Puglia's history takes time," says David. "We are still discovering so much and slowing down will give us time to explore further. This area is magical."

Leonie Whitton & David Westby

Masseria Impisi,
Il Collegio, Contrada Impisi, 72017 Ostuni
- 2 twins/doubles, £50-£70 (min. stay 2 nights);
  2 apartments for 2, £450-£550 per week.
- Dinner with wine, €25, by arrangement
- +39 340 360 2352
- www.ilcollegio.com
- Train station: Ostuni

San Teodoro Nuovo Agriturismo

BASILICATA

The Marchesa's sense of pride in San Teodoro Nuovo is delightfully obvious. Her openness and her enthusiasm for her old family home are palpable. She is from a land-owning family that has had estates in both Calabria and neighbouring Basilicata and wears her considerable family history lightly. Her great grandmother came to this house in 1870 when it was a hunting estate. The Duke and Duchess Marcello and Xenia Visconti di Modrone turned it into a farming estate in the early 20th century. The farm now specialises in organic citrus fruits, wheat, wine and olive oil; they produce their own vegetables, fruit, ricotta, eggs, honey and jam, too. It is best-known, though, as a producer of the best-quality organic table grapes that are sold throughout Europe. This a high-maintenance crop, especially as the grapes ripen, for even a heavy spell of rain can spoil a whole crop.

The rose-tinted house, flanked as it is with bougainvillea and majestic magnolia trees, makes up three sides of a square and is a cool haven from the southern sun. Further relief from the sun is provided by a green sea of citrus and olive groves. You can rent an apartment in a wing of the house, with family antiques and a balcony with tumbling jasmine, or choose one of four beautifully converted ones a short stroll away in the old stables where you can find the restaurant. Every room is elegantly furnished; each has a small parterre garden.

Inside and outside there is a sense of history and place. San Teodoro sits in the middle of Magna Grecia, once under Greek rule and where many majestic sites remain. The main towns of the Magna Grecia are Metaponto, Kroton and Sybaris; the Temple of Hera, just north of nearby Metaponto, is the

most complete of the ruins, with many of its Doric columns still standing.

Maria has added to the family's collection of art and almost every wall could grab your attention. "Our passion for art is fired by the Magna Grecia's rich cultural history," says Maria. "Our chapel in the grounds, in contrast with the house, however, is a simple, sacred space. We hold wedding services there and can welcome up to 100 guests; our family has used it for christenings since my great grandmother's time. There is also a very old cemetery in the grounds that we intend to leave untouched, for to disturb it would disturb the spirit of the place."

There is another family property nearby – a 13th-century castle! Maria's grandmother owned Castello Berlingieri and sometimes pops over with guests on informal visits. "Occasionally it's fun to show people around and we have a picnic in the gardens. They are always thrilled to be taken to a place not normally open to the public."

The bountiful estate produces enough to keep the kitchen staff busy. Your dinner, in the converted-stables restaurant, will be mostly organic produce from the estate or from selected local farms that sell DOP (denomination of protected origin) and IGP (indication of protected origin) produce, such as pepperoni from Senise, beans from Sarconi. "We cook typical Basilicata dishes and we strive to work creatively, discovering new ideas for traditional recipes," explains Maria. "We are proud of our entry in the Slow Food Italy guide and our occasional cookery courses are popular. We explain how we grow our produce, how we prepare our dishes and we dine together. We take participants to local markets and producers, too, to introduce them to local culture." (Alastair's note: we do hope that some of you, our readers, will seize the chance of joining in with these courses.)

The area is popular with artists, and particularly with ceramicists. Grottaglie, to which thousands of Albanians fled in the 15th century after the Ottomans tried to impose Islam upon them, has been the centre of ceramics since the 10th century. The streets are littered with pots and vessels to tempt tourists and it has a famous pottery school, the Instituto Statale d'Arte. Matera is fascinating, too, for its well preserved and very ancient cave dwellings – houses for peasants that were carved out of the steep rock face. The warren-like structures are not unlike Turkey's Cappadocia.

It is good to know that the future for San Teodoro is safe in the D'Oria family's hands. Of Maria's three children, one is in London and two are nearby and Maria is certain that they will, somehow, carry on. "Greeting guests personally and telling them about the history of our home is a gesture that makes a real difference. That is why people come to stay here rather than in a hotel." Indeed, once you have enjoyed San Teodoro it will be hard ever to enjoy anything less lovely.

Marchesa Maria Xenia D'Oria

San Teodoro Nuovo Agriturismo, loc. Marconia, 75020 Marconia di Pisticci
- €120–€140 (€840–€980 per week). Half-board €80–€90 p.p.
- Dinner €25–€30, by arrangement.
- +39 0835 470042
- www.santeodoronuovo.com
- Train station: Metaponto

Hotel Villa Schuler

SICILY

"At the bottom, a high wall and a pink gateway... they were in a delicious garden descending a pergola of roses and grapes. Violets and freesias, geraniums and heliotropes spread in a dazzle of colour and sweetness under gnarled olives and almonds and blossoming plums; stone benches, bits of old marbles, a violet-fringed pool and a terrace leading down to a square white house, a smiling young German girl inviting them in, and then a view – dazzling even to their fatigued, dulled eyes. In front, a terrace, and then nothing but the sea, 700 feet below, the coastline melting on and off indefinitely to the right in great soft curves and upspringing mountains. They would have slept anywhere to belong to that."

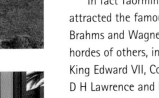

The passage comes from a travel novel written in 1909, called *Seekers in Sicily*, and is a rich description of the Villa which was going strong as a Schuler family-owned hotel even then, at the time when Taormina was already a magnet for sophisticated travellers. From all over the world they came, to the sun-kissed slopes of Mount Etna and history-drenched views over the Bay of Naxos – but equally to the

artists' colony of the town that had been made famous by, among others, Goethe.

In fact Taormina had always attracted the famous – like Brahms and Wagner and, later, hordes of others, including King Edward VII, Cocteau, D H Lawrence and Marlene Dietrich. They still come.

Taormina has suffered a little, of course, from so much attention, and there is little green space left. What is left is the garden of the remarkable Villa Schuler, through which you may stroll up to the famous pedestrian street, the Corso Umberto. I use the word 'remarkable' partly because of the touching way in which the family has managed to hang on to the house despite the appalling vicissitudes of two world wars. It was expropriated in both wars. After the first, local buyers, so pleased that Signor Schuler had returned to buy the house back, withdrew their own bids. After the second, the house was returned to the family, but in grim condition.

So the rebuilding has been painstaking and devoted. What has been recreated is a wonderfully handsome, up-to-date hotel with the charm and elegance of its own past. It is

cool, quiet, impeccably run, with tiled floors, antique furniture and stone balconies on one level and more modern rooms with large terraces at the top. In fact, they are as modern as can be, with WiFi, jacuzzis, and most of the gadgets you could possibly need.

In spite of the part-modernisation, Villa Schuler can claim to be one of the greenest hotels in Italy. Gerhard seems to have thought of everything, so the following may seem like a litany of ecological achievement. But it is worth spelling out, even if briefly:

They have used traditional building methods and natural materials. The ventilation 'system' cunningly uses the up-drafts from the sea. Toxic materials, blithely accepted by most, have been rigorously excluded – even electromagnetic 'smog'. Waste, of course, is separated and recycled to an

"Sun heats the water, local farmers grow much of the food, natural fertilisers nourish the garden"

impressive degree. The sun heats the water, local farmers grow much of the food, natural fertilisers nourish the garden, ecological cleaners are applied to the walls and floors, clever devices will alarm and protect you in case of fire, fossil-fuels are treated with respect and water is conserved. Materials are natural (cotton towels, of course), disposables are reduced to a minimum, and all discarded furniture and equipment is donated to charity. The standards are set at the highest level and the hotel is ISO 14001 certified, which is about as good as it gets. Lastly, all the staff are involved in this commitment.

Gerhard says: "An important part of work has been helping our staff to understand our green philosophy. We encourage them to take their own green actions outside of the hotel, too."

The breakfast of regional specialities is chosen from a menu – rare in Italian places where one

most often finds a buffet. Gerhard has chosen the menu option to make breakfast more relaxing – everything is brought to you – and to minimise waste and packaging; similarly they provide magazines for guests in communal rooms rather than newspapers for there is less to recycle.

It is rare in the world of hotels to find a family so devoted to the family tradition. That, alone, is a seductive feature for those looking for Slow. But the long lazy afternoons in their garden (about which Gerhard and a horticultural expert are writing a book), the views over the sea and to Etna, the deep commitment to running a hotel with the lightest ecological touch – such things are enough to slow a person down.

And the family thrives there: Gerhard's two sons, Alessandro and Andrea, help him and Christine. "We are all totally committed," says Gerhard, "and will always strive to improve."

Christine Voss & Gerhard Schuler

Hotel Villa Schuler,
Piazzetta Bastione, via Roma, 98039 Taormina
- 21 doubles, 5 junior suites, €99–€206.
  Apartment for 2–4, €149–€390.
- Restaurants 100m (special prices for hotel guests).
- +39 0942 23481
- www.hotelvillaschuler.com
- Train station: Taormina-Giardini

Hotel Signum

AEOLIAN ISLANDS

Leave the car behind in Sicily and set off for the island of Salina by boat. The frenetic activity of the port behind you dissolves from the memory as you behold the rugged beauty of the Aeolian island.

Salina, 90 minutes on the ferry from Sicily, is the second largest island in the Aeolian archipelago but only 27km across; you'll be able to borrow or hire bikes to explore. The island, a small patch of land floating in the sea between Naples to the north and Sicily to the south, can claim some fame: *Il Postino* was filmed here. The gentle storyline aroused curiosity all over the world. Nevertheless, the celebrity set and the flash yachts tend to head for the nearby islands of Lipari, Stromboli and Panarea, leaving Salina blissfully peaceful.

It is a volcanic island but the last eruption was a comforting 13,000 years ago, leaving underwater craters that still attract international divers. Naturalists are drawn to the diverse wildlife that lives among the myrtle and broom and forests of poplars and chestnuts. The coastal lake at Lingua in the south was a salt pan and sea salt was the island's main export – now replaced by capers, olives and the sweet Malvasia wine.

Salina, unlike many other small Italian communities, sees very little leakage of youth and talent to cities. Might family-run hotels be pivotal to the success of thriving communities? If so, the Signum can take some of the credit. The owners employ up to 30 staff in the summer and their philosophy of working with local fishermen, farmers and producers fuels the local economy. Clara Rametta-Caruso, Signum's owner and matriarch, feels that the island is a vibrant community and that the young have a sense of place, of belonging.

"There are only 2,500 people on the island so everybody knows everybody. The children like that, not resent it, and want to stay on the island and

work. We employ up to 40 people in summer and have more willing workers than we have jobs."

Clara and husband Michele can count on the help of their two children, too. Son Luca already knows a lot about running the hotel; daughter Matina is at Gambero Rosso's school in Rome. She is looking forward to joining her father full-time in Signum's kitchen. "Signum will always be family run," says Clara, "the children have always wanted to be involved."

Salina packs a punch for its size and there is a thriving eco-tourism sector. "Six hotels have now applied for the European ecolabel and we are witnessing something of a revolution," says Clara. "I am on the tourism council and we try to preserve the island, protect it against environmental damage and set up new initiatives. We want to build a sustainable, year-round approach to tourism. Festivals such as the June Caper Festival and the Salina DOC Fest in September bring many people."

The friendly Signum has a special atmosphere that pulls people back again and again. It sits quietly at the end of a narrow lane and you'd hardly guess it was there, a promising start for a Slow destination. Dining on a terracotta terrace with chunky tile-topped tables and colourful iron and wicker chairs, you gaze out over lemon trees to the glistening sea. A winding labyrinth of paths, where plants flow and tumble, leads to simple and striking bedrooms with antiques, wrought-iron beds and starched lace fluttering at the windows. There is a beautiful infinity pool – that view again – or steps down to a quiet pebbly cove.

The Signum Spa uses one of the the island's best natural resources, geothermic waters, for restorative treatments. The waters emerge at a warming 30°C and are full of minerals said to enhance well-being. The Carusos have installed a 19th-century bath tub and a thermal stove inspired by those first used in Lipari 3,500 years ago; massages can, believe it or not, take place on a bed of rose-perfumed sea-salt.

There are lemon scrubs, prickly pear and almond milk baths and orange blossom massage oils to induce further serenity. Swathes of linen fabric divide massage spaces in the tropical garden, and smiling staff further convince you that you have stumbled into a fairytale oasis.

There is a sense of slow organic growth at Signum. They started with 16 rooms in 1988 and have increased the number to 30 by buying old properties nearby. "The feel is of a Borgo - a self-contained village - rather than a hotel," says Clara.

The sense of self-sufficiency can lull you into 'stasis'. You need hardly step outside to experience island life, for with the lovely local staff and exceptional local food, the whole place is infused with Salina's easy-going spirit. You can arrive with a clear conscience, too: if you have no reason to come via Sicily you can just take the train to Naples then hop on a ferry.

Luca Caruso

Hotel Signum,
via Scalo 15, Malfa, 98050 Salina, Aeolian Islands

- 28 doubles, 2 singles, €130-€340.
- Dinner à la carte, €35-€45. Wine from €15.
- +39 0909 844222
- www.hotelsignum.it
- Train station: Milazzo

Italy on a bike

This book would not be complete without extolling the virtues of cycling in Italy...

"More and more people are intrigued by the charm of moving slowly in their moments of relaxation and leisure, on foot, by bicycle. In our society, invaded by engines and enslaved to speed, this is a luxury that makes us feel free, happy and relaxed; it's a way that helps re-establish a relation with oneself and with nature. Thus the trip is a moment of cultural growth, a way to move that is more careful towards the values of the territory and more respectful of its integrity, a way that helps rediscover new landscapes, forgotten and astonishing. This explains the growing interest in the so-called 'smooth mobility'. Italy has hundreds of kilometres of embankment roads and towpaths..."

Thus runs the introduction to Umbria's *Green Heart of Italy* booklet that focuses on the 60-mile long Spoleto to Assisi *'Greenway'*.

Any attempt to change our lifestyle and go more slowly must involve forsaking cars for some of the time and learning to explore new places and new countries by other means. Fortunately, to cycle in Italy is no sacrifice - quite the opposite. The bike gives you new freedoms to explore towns and countryside. Picking up a bicycle even for just a few days will add enormously to your Italian holiday.

And you won't be alone. Wherever it is level you will find numerous everyday cyclists. In the flat lands of the Po Valley - in Mantua, in Modena, in Parma, in Cremona and countless other cities of the plains - you will find the bicycle a standard way of travelling. Ferrara has one of the highest levels of cycling in all of Europe, with a third of everyday journeys in town made by bike. Recreational trails stretch out to the Delta and the Adriatic.

It is usually easy to hire bikes in Italy, and your hotel or the local tourist office should be able to help. For me there is no better way to see a town than to drop off my luggage, jump on a bike and wander freely around the squares and streets. The bicycle gives you range and freedom, is so much less tiring than walking and is an efficient way of carrying things. You also quickly become integrated into the place.

One thing that strikes me about cycling in Italy is how much time I spend just standing around in Piazzas, leaning on my bike, talking to people and absorbing the atmosphere. Another remarkable thing is the number of women cycling: women shopping, with children, elderly women too, and even women in extraordinary furs. Compare that to the more macho cycling culture in Britain.

In some towns you will find a sophisticated system of bike hire from stands scattered around different areas, and most operate on nominal rates for the first hour or so. You can make a journey from one place to the other, walk around the museum, church or park and then pick up another bike for your onward journey. Parma has a fine example of this scheme. It also has a system for trading in motorbikes for electric bikes, which, of course, helps to reduce noise and pollution in the city.

As well as enabling you to get around towns, a bike can take you further afield. In Italy you will find quiet roads and, amazingly, drivers far more courteous than those in the UK. Traffic-free routes are often beautiful as well as interesting. From Lecco along canal towpaths and riverbanks to Milan you use works engineered by Leonardo; from Peschiera di Garda the floodbank paths take you through the remains of the lakes guarding Mantua. The railway cycle path from Calalzo to Cortina through the Dolomites to Dobbiaco is one of the most memorable off-road routes in Europe. If you are fond of tunnels then the magnificent route from Spoleto toward Norcia will be hard to beat when it is finished, especially as its numerous galleria, spiralling inside the mountain, will remain unlit to preserve the atmosphere of the line!

Taking your bike on public transport is relatively easy, too and the use of a bus or train to take you up some of the bigger mountains is wise. For example, if you take public transport from Verona to Brixen, you can reach the wonderful and largely downhill route from the Brenner Pass all the way back down to Lake Garda. There, you can join one of the northernmost sections of the Ciclopista del Sole, Italy's national route that stretches all the way to Calabria and then carries on to Sicily.

You can usually find good information about each cycling route locally. Tourist information offices should be able to give you maps and details of bike hire centres. A few Italian websites do give cycle route information, notably www.ediciclo.it for Emilia-Romagna in bicicletta – Touring Club Italiano; www.turismo.pesarourbino.it for Pesaro and Urbino cycle tour itineraries; www.bicitalia.org; and, best of all, www.vasentiero.it for numerous detailed guides (some in English) by Albano Marcarini who covers walking and cycling routes with equal knowledge and enthusiasm.

John Grimshaw, CBE, President of Sustrans

Italy by train

If you're sick of being herded around airports and have half a conscience about your carbon footprint, travelling to Italy by train is for you. It is not always cheaper, but if you regard the getting there as part of the holiday you'll add a new dimension to your break.

Getting to Italy

It's 10 hours from London's St Pancras to Turin and 14 hours to Venice and Rome. You make your one and only change in Paris. If you're heading to Turin, you can leave London at breakfast time and be in Turin for dinner. The last 1.5 hours is especially magnificent - mountain ranges flit past your window and the descent from the Alps into to the city is memorable. The trains to Venice and Rome are sleepers and adventures in themselves.

Trips from Turin

Head to Levanto and the coastal towns of the Cinque Terre. It's an exhilarating destination for families as there are beaches, restaurants next to the sea, high and low coast paths for walking and boat and train trips from one town to the other.

Culture vultures could head down the west coast line, then hop to Arezzo, Siena, Pisa or Florence. Journeys are cheap and if you've tried to drive around the hinterlands of these cities, you'll appreciate that this is the stress-free option.

Trips from Venice

Head round the coast to Trieste passing the glistening Castello di Miramare, built by Maximilian for his young bride Carlotta. Jan Morris's exquisite book, *Trieste and the Meaning of Nowhere*, should be your companion. When there

you can hop on bike, boat or funicular railway. On your return journey to Venice, stop off at Treviso, Castel Franco Veneto, Vicenza, Padua and Verona for shopping and art.

Trips from Parma

Mantua, Cremona, Ferrara, Faenza and Bologna line the Po Valley and all have a rich heritage of producing quintessential Italian produce: Parma ham, balsamic vinegar, parmesan. 'Eurostar Italia' (not the Eurostar), 'Intercity' and 'Regionale' are the trains you will need; Regionale is cheap and most open to accommodating bikes.

Trips from Sulmona

Reach Sulmona, the centre of Italy's rail network, via Turin or Rome. Both routes reward you with a magnificent entrance into the mountainous Abruzzo. From Sulmona you can reach mountain walks by taking a bus to Scanno. Foodies should take the bus from Sulmona to Pacentro for lunch at Caldoro, one of Italy's most celebrated Slow restaurants. It's a pleasant 1.5-hour amble back to Sulmona through green lanes, fig groves and allotments.

The Terni line speeds you up to Umbria. Villages before L'Aquila, along the Aterno valley, are worth alighting for: Raiano for the San Venanzo Gullies, Fagnano-Campana for the Stiffe caves. Follow the steps of St Francis by walking between the stations of Contigliano and Gréccio.

Trips from Perugia

If you are staying near Trevi or Spello, take the Umbrian Regional branch line from Perugia's Ponte S Giovanni station to Piero della Francesco's home town of Sansepolcro to see his earliest known work, an altarpiece. Fit in a brief stop at Città di Castello to climb the campanile then take an espresso in the buzzy bar below. Also worthwhile is the walk over the hills from Asissi back to Spello; buy a bus ticket at Asissi station's newspaper shop for the short trip up to the start point.

Trips from Rome

Head south from Rome's Termini station to reach Naples within 2 hours; skip the queues by buying tickets in advance. From Naples, avoiding the hawkers and card tricksters within the station, change onto the independent Sorrento railway for Pompeii, Herculaneum, Vesuvius and Capri. Best of all, you avoid the heavily trafficked peninsular road. Or you can go direct to Palermo in Sicily and get an eyeful of beautiful Calabrian beaches before your train shuffles on to the ferry at Italy's toe and you cross the Straits of Messina.

Useful info

Get your hands on a European Rail Timetable, available in UK bookshops and a printed version of the Trenitalia timetable from Italy's main stations. Tourist offices have bus and train timetables and info on walks and bike hire.
www.raileurope.co.uk is the place to book train tickets to Italy; or to book tickets after discussion call + 44 (0)844 8485848.
www.trenitalia.com is the place to book trains within Italy. www.seat61.com is popular with many travellers.

Sue Learner

Sawday's Special Places to Stay series

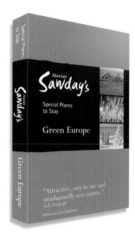

RRP £11.99

Green Europe

Many places call themselves 'eco' or 'green', yet standards differ enormously throughout the world. This guide features very special owners who go the extra mile to provide responsible holidays in Europe. In this new guide you will find special places to stay run by owners who use eco-friendly technologies, contribute to conservation and try to offer something positive to their local communities. There are snow pods, treehouses, yurts, tipis, country B&Bs, organic farmstays and eco-chic hotels. This book also discusses each country's initiatives on 'going green' and provides information on public transport around Europe.

"Sawday is a campaigner for the environment and good food, and his recommendations are like those of a good friend who knows just what sort of place you are looking for." *The Guardian*

RRP £13.99

Green Places to Stay

In this guide we have sought out and visited people with a passion for their local culture and environment, from Borneo to the African savannah. Support local communities and go orca-watching from kayaks, see an underwater ballet of dugongs (sea-cows), go reindeer sledding or rafting down mountains, or find serenity in a reiki course. Find authentic, beautiful places to stay all over the world that use eco-friendly technologies, contribute to conservation and genuinely benefit the local community. Our guide includes treehouses in rainforests, white pods in snowfields, fair trade tented camps, floating eco-lodges, organic mountain farms and eco-chic hotels.

"From remote yurts to treehouses, Green Places to Stay chooses the world's finest." *Wanderlust*

To order call 01275 395431 or visit our online bookshop
www.sawdays.co.uk/bookshop for up to 40% discount

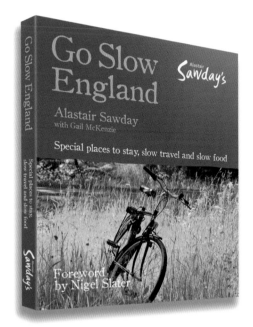

RRP £19.99

Go Slow England

'Slow' embraces an appreciation of good food and artisan producers, of craftsmanship and community, landscape and history. In this guide we have a terrific selection of Special Places to Stay owners who offer a counter-balance to our culture of haste and take their time to enjoy life at its most enriching. You will discover an unusual emphasis on inspiring people and will meet farmers, literary people, wine-makers and craftsmen – all rich with stories to tell.

"*Go Slow England* is our favourite travel book of the year." *Prima*

"*Go Slow England* is a magnificent guidebook." *BBC Good Food Magazine*

"If you need a break from the rat race, you'll find it here." *Waitrose Food Illustrated*

"If one book sums up what life is like outside England's cities, this is it.
It's a homemade-cake-and-jam sort of a book." *Sunday Times Magazine*

**To order call 01275 395431 or visit our online bookshop
www.sawdays.co.uk/bookshop for up to 40% discount**

Place index

Andria
202   Lama di Luna – Biomasseria
Arezzo
118   Agriturismo Rendola Riding
Bibbona
146   Podere le Mezzelune
Borgo San Lorenzo
90   Casa Palmira
Bovara di Trevi
184   I Mandorli Agriturismo
Buonconvento
138   Podere Salicotto
Carpineti
52   B&B Valferrara
Casperia
188   La Torretta
Castel del Piano
176   Villa Aureli
Castellina in Chianti
130   Fattoria Tregole
Castiglion Fiorentino
122   Relais San Pietro in Polvano
Colle di Buggiano
74   Antica Casa 'Le Rondini'
Faédis
48   Casa del Grivò
Figline Valdarno
110   Locanda Casanuova
Fratta Todina
180   La Palazzetta del Vescovo
Greve in Chianti
106   Fattoria Viticcio Agriturismo
Gubbio
168   Locanda del Gallo
Isola del Giglio
154   Il Pardini's Hermitage
Levanto
60   La Sosta di Ottone III
Loro Ciuffenna
114   Odina Agriturismo
Marconia di Pisticci
218   San Teodoro Nuovo Agriturismo
Massa Lubrense
198   Azienda Agricola Le Tore Agriturismo
Mola di Bari
206   Masseria Serra dell'Isola

Montaione
94   Fattoria Barbialla Nuova
Montefiridolfi
102   Azienda Agricola Il Borghetto
Ostuni
210   Masseria Il Frantoio
Ostuni
214   Masseria Impisi
Pierantonio
172   Casa San Gabriel
Pistoia
78   Tenuta di Pieve a Celle
Radda in Chianti
126   La Locanda
Rocca di Roffeno
56   La Piana dei Castagni Agriturismo
Roccatederighi
150   Pieve di Caminino
Sagrata di Fermignano
164   Locanda della Valle Nuova
Salina, Aeolian Islands
226   Hotel Signum
San Quirico d'Orcia
142   Il Rigo
Siena
134   Frances' Lodge
Stazzano
28   La Traversina Agriturismo
Taormina
222   Hotel Villa Schuler
Tavarnelle Val di Pesa
98   Sovigliano
Tortona
32   Agriturismo Cascina Folletto
Toscolano Maderno
36   Agriturismo Cervano B&B
Udine
44   Agriturismo La Faula
Verona
40   Ca' del Rocolo
Vicchio del Mugello
82   Le Due Volpi
Vicchio del Mugello
86   Villa Campestri
Vorno
70   Villa Michaela